A BANTU
IN MY
BATHROOM!

A BANTU
IN MY
BATHROOM!

Debating race, sexuality and other
uncomfortable South African topics

Eusebius McKaiser

BOOKSTORM

ISBN: 978-1-920434-37-3
e-ISBN: 978-1-920434-47-2

First edition, first impression 2012
Second impression 2012
Third impression 2013
Fourth impression 2013
Fifth impression 2018
Sixth impression 2019

First published jointly by
Bookstorm (Pty) Ltd and Pan Macmillan South Africa in 2012

This impression published by Bookstorm (Pty) Ltd in 2018
PO Box 4532
Northcliff 2115
Johannesburg
South Africa
www.bookstorm.co.za

Edited by Sharon Dell
Proofread by John Henderson
Cover design by mr design
Book design René de Wet Designs
Typeset by Lebone Publishing Services
Printed by Pinetown Printers, Pinetown

In loving memory of my mother, Magdalena (Mek) McKaiser.
Death's certainty is the cruellest fact of life.

TABLE OF CONTENTS

Foreword – Jonathan Jansen ix

Introduction 1

Race

A Bantu in my bathroom! 15

Racial baggage in four part harmony 31

Cape Town's dirty, coloured secrets 41

I've even learned Xhosa! 49

Heard the one about blacks who can't be racist...! 63

Affirmative action: a force for good or racism's friend? 71

Sexuality

Not fat enough 85

'Don't you just wanna try, my son? With a woman?' 97

Oh love 113

Of mini-skirts, taxi ranks and sexist pigs 123

There's something I have to tell you 133

If you're a liberal, why don't you like polygamy? 141

Culture

A divided nation 155

The People versus Brett Murray 167

Rhinos are people too 177

Don't call me coconut, bru 189

The funny revolution 201

FOREWORD

If you dare to read this book, protect yourself with a metaphorical condom, for the text is filled with microbial threats to your emotional, spiritual and political health. He writes a fine argument, this native of colonial Grahamstown who grew up in two worlds, one marked by the Settler Monument at the upper end of the town and the other by native locations on the far side of the bridge. But with these fine, microscopic antigens of reasoning he invades our cellular membranes to provoke our most immune beliefs about sex, race, culture and identity in ways one would perhaps expect from such an Oxford-trained philosophy student with a passion for the debating society.

Following a long, tiring week and needing to regain my voice, which had become hoarse after speaking at too many Cape Flats schools, I reluctantly started reading the manuscript after receiving a tight deadline from the publisher for this promised Foreword. Within a minute I was absorbed in the rich, unusual style of writing; within an hour I had finished the work to find myself happy, angry, sad, exhilarated, puzzled and, most of all, amused. Nobody writes like this.

'Like what?' you might ask. A memoir of sorts, but all of us who write stories about others and ourselves consciously and unconsciously decide what to leave out. You do not want to embarrass your family; you know that the more heavy personal reflections on a life should be held back until you enter your 70s; and you try to retain among your readers a measure of respect that would wither if they knew everything about you, from the bedroom to the boardroom.

Eusebius McKaiser has no such scruples, and so you learn in the pacy writing about his rape at the age of seven, his shame at being coloured (he takes this to mean more than a curious, white-initiated classification), and his wild romps in the bedrooms of black men (his preferred 'taste'), making you wonder where the line lies between youthful promiscuity and gay abandon.

The autobiographical introductions to each of his chapters are intended to draw out debate on what Eusebius identifies as a malady of South African thinking on a particular issue. Readers might feel alarmed at his strident arguments, his unforgiving positions, and the way in which he cruelly dismisses opposing viewpoints behind a flurry of rhetoric. No-one is spared, including the writer of this Foreword, and those liberally named (except in one case where, and I have my suspicions, he provides anonymity through the convenience of a pseudonymic reference – 'let's call him Jonathan') may feel a little angry with the misrepresentation of another's standpoint. Still, this writer is at his best when he tells stories, though he loses the plot every time he drifts, annoyingly, into some philosophical abstraction in which he seems to argue with himself.

That said, McKaiser is without question the most exciting and engaging public intellectual in South Africa at the moment. On his radio and television shows – the man keeps moving – he is much more convincing than when he writes. In these media he succeeds in making complex ideas simple and accessible to a wide-ranging audience. He probes with insightful questions rather than insisting on his own opinions. In presenting a social problem he succeeds in drawing out the worst and best from his audiences and has built up a formidable following of listeners with his gentle, prodding and overall progressive views on all kinds of contemporary problems. But the book says as much about McKaiser as it might say about complex issues.

Throughout the volume I felt the sense of an overseas-trained philosopher trying to (re-) discover his country. He pushes a radical liberalism, and sometimes that lands him in trouble, such as in the relentless questioning, on television, of Minister Jeff Radebe. Gone was the reverence and caution of almost every other interviewer; McKaiser let rip and what he did not understand was, one, that Radebe could not follow some of his bullet-fast assertions, arguments and accusations and, two, that this was not the way the Minister was used to being questioned by His Master's Voice. That was the last of McKaiser on that show.

Herein lies a dilemma that many intellectuals face daily. How to entertain power? Whether it be Brett Murray or Jonathan Shapiro or Eusebius McKaiser, liberals and progressives find themselves in trouble by not observing, some would say, that imaginary line between respect and remonstration.

Parenthetically, this appreciation of local context is often very difficult for those of us who lived and trained in long-established democracies where such challenges to power are commonplace and where the language of rights and the value of dissent are ingrained in everyday culture. When we return home, we do not always realise we have been away.

Still, what has become clear in recent times is that this imaginary line exists at different points in the democratic sphere, and that much of our society is still deeply conservative, even regressive, when it comes to the values that should characterise a nation with a progressive constitution. The aggression and contestation that followed 'The Spear'-saga after the public display of the presidential penis in an artwork show just how conflicted we remain about where that line should be drawn.

One of the best responses on this issue came in a recent issue of Justice Malala's Sunday television show, *The Justice Factor*, when he asked a panel discussing 'The Spear'-saga where the line was between freedom of expression and the respect of authorities. The response by journalist Ferial Haffajee was priceless: 'We don't know yet.' And that is why the voice of McKaiser is so critical in this transition to another country – we need to push all the time for the open society and, in doing so, we create the conditions for a more open and tolerant society than the one we have at the moment. Have no fear, this book pushes that line far beyond what many South Africans will feel comfortable with.

I would, of course, have liked the writing to be more generous in its treatment of other beliefs, values and perspectives on the topics surveyed. This does not mean agreement, but it does mean opening up more compassionately the kinds of convictions on which ordinary citizens base their private and public commitments. This surely is a prerequisite for effective pedagogical and political intervention, and transformation, something I draw attention to in *Knowledge in the Blood*. But this is not my book or my voice, and on the landscape of public writers and thinkers here and elsewhere we need the full assortment of approaches to difficult issues in society.

But not only is McKaiser out to discover his country, he is certainly out to discover himself inside his richly hybrid existence. This hybridity and its dilemmas are felt all over the book: a gay man in a straight family; a coloured man in a black/white world; an educated native in an English world; a poor young man in an upper middle class high school and an upper class university community; an African in Oxford. For some strange reason he is sparing of English culture and its institutions, from Rhodes to England proper, as if these all exist, and always existed, in a liberal, non-racial zone of polite innocence; yet he is merciless in his criticism of 'the pitiful underclass' of coloureds, and especially of Cape Town and its 'dirty, coloured secrets'. One has to wonder whether in the quest for 'authenticity', McKaiser has not revealed too much of himself.

What the book does best, however, is to discover us all, for the author brings into his deliberations the voices of ordinary South Africans who speak to him on air or whom he confronts through telephone calls or observes in the parking lots of shopping malls. Our prejudices are laid bare, our defences are taken apart, and our preferences are queried through the stories of his own extraordinary life.

Jonathan Jansen
July 2012

INTRODUCTION

Writing is one of *the* most self-indulgent activities. Anyone who has the audacity to even attempt to write a book is either shamelessly arrogant or blissfully stupid. It takes huge creative effort, and discipline that's in short supply in an age of Twitter and Facebook. It is also, despite many writers' apparent confidence, an emotionally draining activity. Books reflect your inner guts in ways you don't fully control. Even works of fiction – perhaps fiction more so than non-fiction – are nuggets of confessions about your true self. That's where the stupid bit comes in. Writing necessarily means putting a part of your private self out there for affirmation, criticism, engagement, ridicule, judgement.

But when your thoughts have been decently thought through and carefully sculpted, the rewards are immense. I remember the pride I felt when I first saw a full essay of mine in print, in the very first edition of *The Weekender*, a brilliant Saturday newspaper that was prematurely shut down by its owners. I was sitting at a table at Service Station in Melville, Johannesburg, having breakfast with a friend, when I realised the person at the table next to us was reading none other than one Eusebius McKaiser's essay,

'The Oxford blues in black and white'. I desperately wanted him to know that I wrote it; but I simply smiled, faking modesty.

In reality, the writer's ego is gigantic. Mind you, if new parents can brim with pride and joy when spawning a kid, why can't writers feel deep satisfaction when their literary babies are born? Besides, the writer's offspring requires greater skill and creativity. Surely?

I started writing because I was angry. On 1 December 2005 the Constitutional Court declared our existing marriage laws unconstitutional because they discriminated unfairly against gay couples. Everyone who deemed him- or herself progressive was excited. The court gave Parliament one year to change the law so that gay couples could also be allowed to get married. I was furious. Not because I was against gay marriage. But because I was in favour of gay marriage. I didn't think the court's remedy was a good one.

Why should Parliament be given a whole year to change the laws? Why couldn't the court simply say, as it was entitled to, 'From the end of this court session, marriage laws will be understood in sex-neutral terms?' Then gays and lesbians could get married immediately. I was astounded that 'progressives' weren't thinking clearly in their hasty celebration of the judgment.

Imagine a racist law was struck from the statute books but the court had said, 'We give Parliament a year to change the laws so that blacks can also use public facilities.' We would all be up in arms! But of course gay people are not as worthy of immediate justice as black people. There is still a hierarchy of suffering, a hierarchy of victimhood, in our society.

Armed with this anger, I wrote a little polemic, intended as a 'letter to the editor', to *Business Day*. I immediately received a response that almost moved me to tears. Rehana Rossouw, who was in charge of the opinion pages at *Business Day*, stopped the paper from going to press, having instantly decided that my piece should be run the following day as the main opinion piece. She recognised not just the freshness of the argument – a liberal critique of what seemed like a liberal judgment – but she said she also liked my passion, my writing. Until then I never thought I could seriously write features or essays. I was happy, as a sort of professional competitive debater, that I could speak very well, and persuade audiences through the spoken word. Rehana nurtured me as a writer, however, and gave me generous space in *The Weekender* which she went on to edit.

Rehana is not responsible for my literary and argumentation weaknesses, or my often biting interventions in public debate that irritate many of you. But I am grateful that, like a selfless older sister, she helped me realise that there's more to my communicative armoury than the spoken word. I am now, many years later, addicted to writing. If I had a choice between never again being able to speak to audiences, and never again being able to write for public consumption, I would choose spontaneous combustion. It is an unconscionable choice. Both are now part of my DNA.

THE PLACE OF WRITERS AND ANALYSTS IN AN AGE OF SOCIAL MEDIA

I love social media. And I hate social media.

Social media produced several valuable changes in public dialogue. First, it has democratised public debate. Everyone can put an opinion out there, and that's a good thing.

Second, and related to my first point, it has weakened the role of the gatekeeper of traditional debate platforms like print media outfits. Who cares anymore if an editor of a newspaper hates your guts? You can put your article on a blog, and send out the link as a tweet immediately. Editors, and section editors of big titles, have far less power now than they did even three years ago. That's a very good thing. They now have to get over being far less important, and they have to work harder to be respected.

Third, accountability has been enhanced. You instantly know when you've dropped the ball as a writer, talk show host, politician, public servant, or even as an active tweep. People are often vicious and unkind on social media platforms, but instant feedback and engagement with the general public is a good thing. It breaks down the unnecessary barriers between newsmakers and opinion shapers and those being written about or those who have decisions made for them.

But I also hate social media. The flip side of the democracy coin is zero quality control. Not every opinion is equally valid, equally informed, equally coherent. It can be very frustrating spending huge amounts of serious time reflecting on an issue, and having unconsidered responses dominate the debate about your work. Worse, personal attacks and insults can go unchecked. And they can sting. You can even be insulted for not wanting to engage with the insults! So there are days when I miss the traditional gatekeeper. Yet, this is probably a price worth paying for democratising public debate.

This brings me to the question of whether or not social and political analysts are even necessary these days. Do they – we – still have a place in an era when anyone can, and everyone tends to, opine online? The answer is 'yes', but we have to work harder to be relevant, just as an editor has to work harder to be taken seriously as an important figure in public life.

There is just no way Twitter and Facebook could be decent substitutes for longer pieces of writing, and for more nuanced public debates, like seminar-series pieces. Social media platforms, in their current form, are still too limited. I tried using Twitter, for example, to see if I could extend some of my journalistic work. And I had limited success. I managed, for example, to expose a politician for not knowing as much as she ought to about a public health debate. I also managed to learn some amazing biographical facts about a local comedian I had twitterviewed. So the platform has some value: it is good for news transmission; it is good for branding; it is good, in a limited way, for quick dialogical sparring.

But on Twitter you could never properly hammer out all the legal or moral dimensions, for example, of a public health debate. Facebook is marginally better, but here it depends on the goodwill and consistency of your Facebook friends, and their willingness to dig deep and engage each other in an evidence-based manner. Sometimes they do; often they don't.

The bottom line is that these technologies, as invasive as they are, do not displace the traditional role of a social or a political analyst. The analyst's role is similar to that of the artist: to interrupt and disrupt social life with sincere, considered observations, comments and arguments about yourself and your society. The intellectual and moral burden that flows from this is to read widely, to think seriously, to engage others' work generously and fully, and to pay close attention to the quality of your own interventions. Entertaining and famous social media stars are not, in this sense, real social and political analysts. They are just famous, and at best should be described, maybe, as commentators, since they comment without feeling the intellectual burden that a committed analyst ought to feel.

Analysts now need to learn to promote their work within the realities of shifting patterns of human behaviour. Any writer or analyst, who wants to be relevant, must be active online. That's non-negotiable.

The greatest challenges, however, are around style and tone. While many people are still willing to read traditional forms of writing, attention spans aren't what they used to be. Pieces that are accessible, funny, filled with stories and anecdotes, are far more likely to gain traction on the internet than ones that are simply lifted from a traditional print media outfit and put online. So the styles of the works that we write now need to take into account the casual online behaviour of readers. You need to draw readers in by locating yourself in their world. That is tough. It means that analysis cannot only be about me, the writer.

In this collection of essays I was mindful of this challenge. It caused me sleepless nights. How do you write so that a professor can be challenged by the complexity and nuances of your ideas and, yet, stylistically, you get those ideas out there in such a way that someone with little formal education can also engage with you? That is bloody hard, and a writing skill very few have. The truth is that some academics cannot write for the public. That's nothing to be ashamed of. It is a unique skill.

Although, that said, I sometimes think South African academics deliberately do not write clearly, and don't want the public to understand their ideas. And that is only slightly cheeky: as soon as people understand your jargon, they are able to engage with you and show up the weaknesses in your position. Some academics probably don't want to be engaged, don't want to be shown up! Academia is often seen as only for really clever people. It is, actually, also a safe place for people who are terribly scared of public debate.

Ironically, many South African columnists are hugely popular, and revered by readers, despite their ideas sometimes being very pedestrian. But, they can be understood. And readers reward clarity.

I wanted to have my cake and eat it. I refuse to pretend I did not have a great formal education, having studied law and philosophy, and having lectured philosophy. Yet, at the same time, I take offence at the suggestion that one cannot write about complex ideas and arguments in a way that can be accessible for people with less formal education than oneself.

So this collection is my own experiment in style. I have drawn a lot on anecdotes and personal stories, and have tried to drop academic jargon and style, and yet I am hoping the final product is a collection of essays that everyone – from my radio listeners, to kids in my poor community where I was raised, my relatives and academically gifted and pretentious, brilliant friends of mine – can enjoy, agree with, disagree with, and deem a worthwhile effort.

SO WHAT IS THIS COLLECTION ABOUT?

My two essayist heroes are George Orwell and James Baldwin. I only really discovered, to my embarrassment, Orwell-the-essayist after not returning to my friend, the frightfully clever Lwandile Sisilana, his book, *Shooting the Elephant.* It is a collection of some of Orwell's best essays, including the one which gives the collection its title. Orwell's single most attractive literary feature, for me, is his ability to write plainly, yet without loss of insight.

The lesson of his work is that one can observe and convey an observation, without getting trapped in the pretence of fanciful words and sentences. Insights, and thoughts, should determine word choices. Too often, stale words and phrases determine what we say, what we write. When we allow that, we actually stop thinking, and just babble. In fact, this book itself is littered with stale words and phrases and every time I typed one I felt like I had let myself down (like when I typed, 'I wanted to have my cake and eat it' a little earlier). When I do that I feel like I deliberately put on dirty socks that smell because I am too lazy to fetch fresh ones from the washing line outside. (See, now *there's* a fresh analogy.) When I grow up, I want to write like Orwell.

As for James Baldwin, I fell in love with that ugly man while living in England. His writing is as gorgeous as he was not. I love his work so much that I genuinely get annoyed when I see other fools claiming him as one of their favourite writers. Just the other day on Twitter, someone agreed with me that Baldwin is brilliant, and rattled off their favourite Baldwin novels. I hated that tweep. It was like reminiscing about my favourite lover only to discover that all along I had been madly in love with a philanderer who had cheated on me. But brilliant literature should be widely read. And grudgingly I accept that it is unsurprising that every Tom, Dick and Harry wants to impress in a virtual conversation by name-dropping 'James Baldwin'.

One of his works that sparked my interest in essay writing many years ago was *Notes of a Native Son*. (And, for the record, the use of the word 'bantu' in the title of my book is not a literary allusion, before anyone with a post-modern bent gets excited!) I cannot comprehend how a 21-year-old human being could be capable of so much insight into humanity, into the proverbial human condition. That is how old Baldwin was when he published this collection of essays. What gripped me about the collection, however, was not so much the literary quality – although that is worth appreciating – but the profound honesty of the work. Baldwin draws a lot on his personal life and uses his personal life to comment on his society. That is a technique that appeals to me. It is also emotionally a gamble. In a country, like ours, where you can either get excessive sympathy – 'ag shame!' – or be hit with blunt verbal objects – 'your work is k*k!' – writing about your life means even more potential emotional rewards, but also potential emotional abuse. I have taken that risk in this book, as you will find out very quickly.

I took the risk because I want to be a half decent essayist. That requires honest writing, personal writing. This is not a collection of column entries. They attempt to be essays in the classic sense of the word. You can judge the quality of the writing, and of the arguments, the observations, but that was the literary aim. Nothing in here has been previously published. One reason is that I regard it as scandalous that someone can call themselves an author after googling their previously published columns, and sticking these in one book. Another reason is that, frankly, no local print outfit allows long form writing. So even if I wanted to catalogue essays, I couldn't. I haven't really written essays before, because the local media space does not allow writers to do so. I wish that would change.

The themes of these essays preoccupy my intellectual and personal life: race, sexuality and culture. I grapple at length in the first section with racialism, racism and the moral and policy questions that come out of our socially constructed identities. In one essay, for example, I insist we all have more racial baggage than we care to admit ('Racial baggage in four part harmony') while in another I write, for the first time, about coloured identity, in a very personal sketch ('Cape Town's dirty, coloured secrets'). This section highlights many other issues that we inevitably dissect when we talk and debate race, and includes a principled defence of affirmative action ('Affirmative action: a force for good or racism's friend?').

The section on sexuality is naturally the most personal. I share my dad's reaction to finding out that I am gay ('Don't you just wanna try, my son? With a woman?'). I also try to make sense of our violent sexualities and misogyny ('Of mini-skirts, taxi ranks and sexist pigs'). There are other interventions, also, including a provocative and sceptical view of love ('Oh love') and an argument for why polygamy is acceptable ('If you're a liberal, why don't you like polygamy').

A wide range of essays appear in the final section on culture, including a defence of Brett Murray's right to produce bad and offensive artwork ('The People versus Brett Murray'). I had great fun denying that we are, or need to be, a united country ('A divided nation') but end on a positive note with a tribute to our brilliant local stand-up comedians, reflecting on their role in our fractured society ('The funny revolution').

Some of the material in this book will, I think, for some people, be troubling: aesthetically (sex is not for everyone), morally (defending polygamy might upset you deeply) and intellectually (it insists on being argument-rich but refuses to bow to academia's techniques). My only duty, however, is to write sincerely. And that has been achieved. I think?

race

IS IT MORALLY ACCEPTABLE TO STIPULATE THE
COLOUR OF YOUR HOUSEMATE?

IS IT REALLY POSSIBLE TO LEAVE YOUR
PRIVATELY-HELD VIEWS ON RACE AT HOME?

ARE WE REALLY PREPARED TO ACCEPT THE
REQUIREMENTS OF A NON-RACIAL DEMOCRACY?

A BANTU IN MY
BATHROOM!

Last year I came across an interesting ad in *The Star* while searching for accommodation. The person who placed the ad was willing to share her house with a stranger. But it was the description of the preferred lodger that *really* caught my attention. The advertiser – call her Sally – made it clear that she was looking for a white person.

I could not resist. I picked up my phone and called her.

'Hi there. Is that Sally?!'

'Yes it is!' a rather friendly voice answered. She could not possibly be racist, I thought. Racists can't be so jolly, surely?! Racists are supposed to be angry and have heavy Afrikaans accents. This woman did not sound like someone whose late husband wore khaki shorts. She sounded like someone who could make us cute little cucumber sandwiches and a fresh pot of Earl Grey tea – using tea leaves. She could have been Mrs Higgins, the wonderful old white lady who taught me to play the piano at primary school – St Mary's Primary, for poor coloured kids in Grahamstown. And, like Mrs Higgins, I imagined Sally owned a bicycle with a square, brown basket at the front, which she cycled around her quiet neighbourhood, especially when she needed to go to a grocer to stock up on Earl Grey tea leaves.

But, of course, it is difficult to recognise a racist only by the tone of their voice, so it would be unfair of me to deprive Sally of a chance to defeat a stereotype. Non-racists do not have a monopoly on being jolly. Besides, it didn't help that I was 'speaking well'. At any rate, I shouldn't be hasty with character judgements on the basis of a phone chat. I needed to hear a bit more.

'I'm phoning about the room that you advertised? I came across the advert in *The Star* and was wondering whether the room is still available?'

'Oh yes it is! Are you interested?'

Wow, how welcome can one be? Is the company of the family cat that tiresome after all those decades of unconditional love and dedicated companionship? Is the little puss no longer good enough as an old white lady's best friend?

'I am interested, yes! I have been looking to move to Sandton 'cause it is closer to work. But ... I'm not white, my dear. Do I have to be white?!' (I suspect it is not necessary to confess parenthetically that I was having soooo much fun.)

'Yes, as the advert said!' There was a slight but noticeable shift in her tone now. A hint of irritation could be detected miles away and the possibility of a khaki-clad husband, still alive and well, could no longer be ruled out. In fact, I imagined a man called Gert sitting in the background, reading the back pages of *Beeld*, lowering the newspaper, and looking *beswaard* ('gravely concerned' in the most Afrikaans way possible; *'beswaard'* is an emotion uniquely felt in the language and being of Afrikanerdom). I was on a roll now and decided to go for gold!

'Don't you think that's a little bit racist?' I asked.

'Not at all! I just want to live with people of my kind! People I can relate to! What's wrong with that?'

A fair response, perhaps? I wasn't so sure. So I continued for a little while longer. I had nothing else to do that morning; no Earl Grey tea to serve visitors at my end.

'But what does race have to do with getting along with someone? How do you know that your next best friend will NOT be a black person? You can't know just by looking at someone's skin colour whether or not you will get along with them, surely?'

'You clearly have a chip on your shoulder!' she snapped back. At this point I realised that she would make for a wonderful guest on my radio show. I started regretting not recording our exchange.

'I am a talk show host at Talk Radio 702, ma'am and would like to ... ' and before I could finish she hung up. I was left with a naughty smirk on my face and my brain went immediately into 'so-what-does-it-all-mean?' mode.

I decided to share the anecdote with listeners of my weekly radio programme *Politics and Morality* on Talk Radio 702. I posed the question, 'Is it racist to rent your room only to persons of a particular race group?' It was one of the most revealing conversations I've had with a radio audience.

It goes without saying that each radio station – in fact, each show on a radio station – has a specific profile of listeners who self-select that station or slot. So I know we cannot draw easy generalisations about the entire country based on the viewpoints of one radio station's callers. In fact, one can't even take those who call in during a particular time slot as representative of all those who are listening to that particular slot! But from somewhere deep inside my gut (if that counts for anything?), I suspect that the discussion which followed did probably reveal truths about most of us. Social scientists, of course, might have other thoughts. Anyway, here is what happened on radio that night.

There was a broad convergence in opinion among my listeners, black and white. The majority thought that it was *not* racist to have a racial preference for a tenant.

One group of listeners thought that since the property was privately owned, Sally could do whatever the heck she wanted to do with it so long as she did not break any general laws of the land. For this group, Sally's preference was no different from someone who wanted to live only with non-smokers. It was not even a question of whether Sally's attitude was justified. It was simply her *right* to have this attitude, finish and *klaar*!

A second group had a somewhat more complicated position. This group thought that if Sally had a flat or cottage in her yard and only wanted whites to live in it then she really would be a racist. However, from my description of the advert it was clear that we were talking about a room in the main house. That, apparently, changed everything. Your own house is a much more intimate, private space than a cottage on your property that you're not living in yourself. And so Sally should be let off the hook for having race-specific preferences in her choice of housemate.

These arguments fascinated me. I was desperately trying to make sense of our racialism, and attitudes towards others, in this conversation. I disagree profoundly with both sets of opinions and wrestled with my callers for almost two hours. I understood where they were coming from but could not quite put my finger on a deep discomfort I felt with their convictions, especially those who fell into the 'in-my-backyard-perhaps-but-NOT-in-my-house!' category. As is often the case with live radio discussion, the most precise language often only hits you after the fact. While I put up a good fight challenging my listeners, it was only really in the days and weeks afterwards that I figured out what had bothered me. The attitudes which lurked beneath those seemingly reasonable and innocent arguments were morally odious. When those underlying attitudes are fully excavated and closely examined, they betray a deeply ingrained and objectionable racialism – and sometimes outright racism – many years after democracy's birth. I believe that those callers who argued that what happens behind the walls of private property is not up for moral evaluation, are just not thinking carefully.

First, let me make an important concession. There is definitely something both tempting and intuitively right about the claim that we all need a break from the burden of social and moral rules. Our private lives, including decisions about who we let into our homes, must be allowed to be beyond the wagging finger of moralists. 'Allow us to be racist at least on our own turf!' a choir of Save Our Sally (SOS) members might shout. To shout back 'No!' seems hasty.

There is something to be said for protecting the private space from public morality. If we value individuality and authenticity, as we surely must if we are to take seriously the meaning and point of liberal pluralism, then we must allow for conditions under which all of us can peacefully co-exist with maximum opportunity to be our true selves.

And, if your true self is someone who only wants to break croissants with whites (or only eat pap and chakalaka with blacks) then society must put up with those preferences. That is logic that I get, with which I agree for the most part, and which I am happy to attribute, in the non-white spirit of Ubuntu, to those Sally supporters who argue for her entitlement to do as she pleases with whomever, and on, her property.

But there is a difference between the *right* to rent your room to whites only and our entitlement to judge your actions *morally*. We do not think that a woman's right to marry a misogynist bastard means we cannot criticise her decision. We do not think that a gardener's right to accept his employer's insistence on being called '*baas!*' and his employer's right to offer premium wages for being called '*baas!*' mean that we cannot evaluate the moral quality of that relationship. And many of us seem to think that the right of a millionaire to display his or her wealth ostentatiously does not mean they are immune to moral comment. Remember, for example, the uproar when businessman Kenny Kunene threw lavish parties – he was criticised for behaviour that some regard as immoral even though he has a right to throw lavish parties.

Morality follows us just about everywhere, and so I don't think we can simply say that just because Sally has a right to live with whomever she wants, and just because she should in general be given space to live a life she chooses for herself, that we cannot ever raise moral questions about her private choices. We can, and this ad I stumbled upon seems a perfect case in a country with our racial history, about which to ask probing questions about the motives behind these preferences, their origins and their content. So her domestic preferences are fair game.

Besides, I seriously doubt that Sally regards herself as acting immorally. Only someone who is genuinely amoral would truly not care about the moral quality of her actions, let alone what the rest of us have to say about it. Sally does care.

Sally was happy to engage me and offer reasons for her actions. She was implicitly accepting that she could be criticised but thought she had a sufficient defence for her racialised preferences. She is not a hermit. She is not a sociopath. She lives in society. She is of society. I therefore reject the all-too-easy (though tempting and seemingly reasonable) claim that how we behave privately and what we do with our private property cannot and should not be morally probed. It can and it should.

And if we had a chance to meet Sally, I suspect she would agree, but simply say her preferences *are* morally acceptable. Well, are they? Before answering this question, there is one more aspect of Sally's case that I want to comment on and which complicates the racial preference debate.

It crystallises around a recent visit from a friend of mine, John, who now lives in Oxford.

John was fascinated when I told him about the advert saga and the radio discussion it spawned. Being a near perfect human being, the original 'Mr Nice Guy', John confessed that when he had been on the lookout to share a house with someone in Oxford, he declined an opportunity to live with a disabled person. He did not think he could live with someone who had a serious physical disability. Agreeing to live with such a person he felt would effectively mean agreeing to take on a certain kind of responsibility, which he felt he was not capable of fulfilling. He had no prior relationship with the person and this lessened the emotional stakes somewhat when it came to turning down the offer.

Of course, he felt horrible about the decision because it felt callous. But it was an honestly-made decision. It was based on truthful self-evaluation of what kinds of living arrangements were comfortable for John. And that, surely, is okay? We cannot be expected to be moral saints. This is also why it is okay, too, to simply not want to live with someone who is a smoker, say. But these factors – Am I ready to be a quasi-carer for a disabled housemate? Can I put up with puffs of smoke? – are not signs of a bad moral character, suggested John. They are simply a combination of satisfying one's arbitrary preferences ('I don't like smoke!') and considering practical facts ('I just won't be able to cope with negotiating the needs of a disabled housemate.')

I'm not convinced that Sally's preference is in the same category as these preferences. And it is, at any rate, debatable whether John's attitude towards disability is acceptable, even if someone's irritation for smoke is acceptable. These cases are too different to be treated in the same way, but there is something to be learned from the differences, and the false appearance of salient similarities. Is it possible, if we get back to Sally, that there is nothing more to Sally's preference than convenience? John finds it inconvenient to live with a disabled person. Let's say you find it irritating to smell smoke. So is there not simply a similar kind of inconvenience that Sally will experience in being 'forced' to live with a non-white person?

I hope no-one finds this line of reasoning compelling enough to let Sally off the hook. My skin colour is not a disability. It is an arbitrary difference between me and Sally. And so it is not clear to me that Sally would be inconvenienced by a black skin in her house in a way that can seriously be regarded as too high a burden for anyone to bear. If I was judging Sally for not adopting twenty orphans, I think one could easily make a case for why it would be acceptable for the inconvenience of such an adoption to be a reason for Sally to politely decline. But my skin colour? The analogy between the disabled lodger and a black lodger is therefore unconvincing. (I will leave aside another response to John, of course, which is to challenge his assumptions about disabilities, and what exactly the 'burdens' would be living with a disabled person. I have no doubt that millions of self-sufficient disabled persons would rightly take deep offence at the suggestion that they are an inherent burden on abled-bodied persons. All that is important here, for my purposes, is for us to recognise that when someone says she only wants to live with white people in her house, she can't justify that preference by saying it is 'inconvenient' to have a black person around. That is an honest response, perhaps, but a morally impotent one. In fact, one might even doubt the supposed honesty and innocence of the 'inconvenience' argument: racism is often the operating motive, but how many of us are capable of admitting to *that* kind of motive?)

So where does all of this leave the first batch of my callers who suggested that it is Sally's house, and so she can choose her tenant. I hope the arguments I have introduced make it clear why that is at the very least a hasty response from my listeners. In short, yes, Sally has a right to live only with white people but the fact that she has a right to make a random decision of this kind does not mean we can't judge the way she exercises that right.

The more difficult, and much more important, question is ultimately whether there is something wrong with the preference itself? Is there something wrong with Sally wanting to live only with whites? After all, there are many preferences we have in life that are arbitrary, and acceptably so. I do not have to justify why I prefer white meat to red, Bon Jovi to Simphiwe Dana, Chopin to Mozart, Johannesburg to Cape Town, bulkier men over scrawny ones. So if there is so much in the rich texture of our lives that are merely preferences, the ingredients of our individual personalities and idiosyncrasies, then surely that can straightforwardly extend to preferences about the race of persons with whom we share a house? No?

I find it hard, I must admit, to be too prescriptive about what things should guide people's preferences. But if we can have critical conversations about the basis of our preferences, then surely we should? I do not know the details of Sally's preferences because we did not have a chance to take our conversation further, but I think we can make some reasonable guesses if we place her life within the socio-political context of our country. We live in a country in which all of our lives are racially saturated from a young age; this is particularly true of South Africans who grew up during apartheid. Sally is one such South African. It is very likely that she internalised the racial hierarchy of apartheid that assigned certain roles to different race groups and instilled in whites a sense of superiority and in blacks a sense of inferiority. We were legally forced, as members of different race groups, to live apart in geographically segregated areas. We socialised in reasonably homogenous groups for a large period of time. It goes without saying that as both co-conspirators and victims of this system many of us hardened our attitudes towards members of other groups.

So on the one hand, there is a certain kind of innocence about the preference that Sally expresses. It really just might stem from the way she was socialised, and she merely wishes for maximum comfort in her own home. That seems perfectly reasonable to me.

On the other hand, the origins of the preference are morally odious. The preference is the product of our racist past. And there is the conundrum: if I know that preferences stem from a morally odious past, should I not find ways to rid myself of those preferences, provided that it is possible to do so? This is difficult. The argument is only persuasive, I admit, if someone accepts that preferences that stem from a racist past should be eliminated. And it is not clear that there is a duty to do so.

I would therefore criticise Sally's preferences, still, but in a qualified way: Sally's racialised preferences are the product of a racist past and are therefore morally odious. But Sally does not have a strict duty to now get rid of those preferences as an adult since no one is demonstrably harmed by those preferences. However, to the extent that Sally accepts that she shares the goal of a non-racial, democratic South Africa, she might want to reflect on what steps she could take to begin to chip away at the enduring nature of her racialised preferences – steps that will involve now getting to know 'the other'.

That, to me, seems like a more careful reaction to Sally's preference than the crude, 'It is her home!' retort of many of my callers.

So what then of the second batch of callers who thought it would only have been racist for Sally to object to blacks in a cottage in her garden? When the second group made that distinction between the flat in the yard (which they think Sally should be comfortable renting to Sipho) and the main house (from which Sipho can be excluded) they betrayed dark secrets about themselves and our country.

Firstly, this viewpoint is an acknowledgment (indeed, an expression) of deep racial angst. Why else would you be fine with Sipho sleeping in the flat outside but heaven forbid that you should wake up in the morning and the first thing you see on your way to the bathroom is the heart attack-inducing spectacle of Sipho smiling at you, a horror that just might elicit a scream of apartheid proportions, 'Help! There is a Bantu in my bathroom!'

There was an eeriness about the calm with which this group of Sally-supporters made the distinction between a flat in the yard and the main house; a kind of unreflective, resigned acceptance that racial angst is a mundane truth that is to be accommodated – though, of course, in the backyard only, not in my father's house!

Secondly, there is no appetite here for extinguishing this racialised preference. No-one ever asked what Sally might do to overcome her insistence that only whites could be housemates. I was robustly engaged for daring to criticise what someone does with their private property. I was robustly engaged for not appreciating how a room in a house – as opposed to a flat in a yard – makes all the moral difference in our choices of who to live with!

Yet, not one listener, black or white, displayed the same robustness towards Sally. No-one grappled with how it is that eighteen years after our democratic journey had started, race-specific friendship preferences (which, by her own admission, was the basis of Sally's search for a white housemate) could still endure uncritically. Indeed, the question did not even arise for my listeners. Racialism, it seems, has become something of an enduring meme.

Not that I am a proponent of non-racialism; rather, I was fascinated by the deep inconsistency that South Africans display. Racialism, by the way, simply means that we recognise racial differences, usually on the basis of skin colour, hair texture, and other observable traits. It is unscientific, of course, but that is true of many other socially constructed categories also. We can and do 'see' race. Racism is something else: it is when you go a step further, using racial differences as a basis of unfair discrimination, going from 'seeing' race (racialism) to being prejudiced (racism). In contexts that are less personal (such as public debate about voting preferences), the same group of radio listeners are quick to bemoan racialism's reach and endurance. But racialism's reach and endurance inside their homes and hearts dare not be spoken about. Why can you complain so easily, in disbelief, about people with racial political preferences, but defend your right to have exclusively racial preferences when it comes to your friends? This is a tragic lack of self-examination.

The discussion confirmed just how deeply ingrained racialism is in our collective social psyche. Sally's advert was not an exceptional affair. She was simply being honest and giving public expression to familiar, widespread racialism that can be easy to miss because it tends to be, for the most part, non-violent, privately-held and expressed away from the glare of public scrutiny. Sally is ultimately one of us. We cannot disown her.

Most importantly, and most tragically of all, is the failure of too many South Africans to see the intimate links between the private and public spheres. If you cannot imagine being best friends with someone of another race group, if you cannot imagine sharing a house with someone of another race group, then how on earth do you think racial tension at work and in public spaces will ever be dealt a death blow? The very same radio listeners fighting for Sally's right to display racialism privately are the ones who jam the phone lines in discussion and debate about race-based public policies like affirmative action and black economic empowerment.

'How do you think we will ever achieve a non-racial South Africa if we still use race categories?!' they will ask me rhetorically. Yet, the same old race categories are allowed, without a hint of self-criticism, let alone a hint of irony, to influence their most personal choices.

Clearly our private actions and attitudes provide a much more honest test of where we are at in terms of racial integration than does our willingness to participate in rainbow nation acts in the workplace or in a sports arena. Also, the amount of effort we put into eliminating racism (or racialism, if that is your goal also) in our *private* lives will also partly determine how successfully, and how quickly, we do so in the public sphere. *This causal connection between the domestic and public spheres is lost on too many South Africans.*

There are two insights we must take to heart: one is that we should be on the lookout for sophisticated tactics we all use (often subconsciously) to mask racism and racialism, such as seemingly innocent explanations for counter-productive attitudes and choices – 'It's simply a matter of taste (or preference or randomness) that Sally does this or that!'; the other, and perhaps more important, conclusion is that we need to appreciate how public racism, and racialism, are in part sustained by what we do or do not do in the privacy of our homes. We take our private racism, and our private racialism, into the public space. We therefore cannot make progress in the public space without fixing what we do in private.

Non-racism, and non-racialism, begins at home.

**DOES OUR OUTRAGE OVER OTHERS' RACISM
NOT MASK OUR OWN PREJUDICES?**

ARE YOU IN DENIAL?

IS JESSICA DOS SANTOS AN ALIEN, OR ONE OF US?

RACIAL BAGGAGE IN FOUR PART HARMONY

SKETCH ONE:

A couple of days ago I had a rather embarrassing experience. I was sitting at one of my favourite spots in Rosebank – popular coffee shop Ninos – overlooking the parking lot while waiting for my creative juices to kick in after a bout of writer's block. I got distracted by some noise, and looked up. Two women seemed to be having a fairly tense conversation. One of them seemed to have bumped the other's car. I didn't see the accident, so had no clue which one of them might have been in the wrong. As they exchanged numbers, their conversation, judging by the increasingly wild gesticulation, seemed to be getting more heated.

I instinctively found myself silently egging on the black lady, as one might anxiously hold thumbs for your favourite boxer in the ring. The Indian lady seemed louder – I could certainly hear her voice more clearly – and this made me nervous about whether or not my player in the road rage match was going to win the verbal warfare. But alas, the black lady, though also talking a lot, seemed more timid, and so I feared that she might come out of it all the worse for wear.

Why, you might wonder, did I instinctively side with her? Simply because she was black. I did not know her. I might never even meet her. For all I know, she could have been in the wrong, and hurled abuse at her Indian counterpart, thus deserving those loud protests. Yet, the fact that she was black was enough for her to get my sympathy and all my goodwill. There was no sympathy or goodwill, I'm afraid, for the person who looked less like me, the Indian lady.

SKETCH TWO:

A good friend of mine, Seth, confessed to me many years after we first met that he had a rather horrible thought the first time he saw me. He walked into my philosophy tutorial at the beginning of his university career and when he realised that I was the tutor, he thought, 'Oh dear, my luck to be assigned the incompetent black tutor.' That is the sort of confession one can only trot out if your friendship is more solid than the skull of a politician. I chuckled, and we laughed it off over a pint of lager – or three.

We didn't need to analyse the confession. It was obvious what was going on: my skin colour was assumed to be carrying information about me. And in this case, my black skin carried the warning, 'incompetent!' The onus was on me to disprove the assumption. Only white tutors could be assumed to be competent unless proven to be useless. It was the other way round for black tutors.

SKETCH THREE:

Jessica dos Santos is a name we didn't really know until early May 2012, but now her story has been filed in the annals of Twitter infamy. She is a white model who had an unfortunate encounter with a black guy who reportedly made unwelcome and unacceptable sexual advances towards her. She was so angry that she tweeted about the 'kaffir'. She was quickly, and ferociously, sanctioned by almost every South African on Twitter. One magazine, *FHM*, almost instantly stripped her of some title she had won under their banner, and made it clear they would never work with her in future. She experienced the virtual equivalent of having a ton of rotten tomatoes thrown at her.

Not even a breakfast function at which she attempted to reconcile with another thoughtless tweep, a black woman who retorted with unacceptable racism (suggesting that whites ought to have been killed), could salvage her bruised image. She became the symbol of all unexpressed and latent racism that might exist in every nook and cranny in our country. And everyone wanted to prove their progressive credentials by venting more angrily than other tweeps.

I encountered at least two responses that typified the engagement with Dos Santos's racism. One Facebook friend of mine gave me advice on my way to a recording for a television show on which I had been invited to appear to speak about the incident and its aftermath. My Facebook friend urged me to remind *'these* racists' that their racism was disgusting and that 'they' had no place in our society.

At a friend's birthday braai, the incident, inevitably, also became a topic of discussion at some point in the afternoon. One guest lamented, 'You know, I almost feel sorry for that white girl. She must have been raised in an incredibly closed and insulated community.'

The reactions of the online masses, and the reactions of my Facebook friend and my friend's braai guest, are intriguing: they suggest that racists are not us. Racists are alien. They are outliers in our society. They are not typical. They are a freak fact of our lives. If we could get rid of the three racists spoiling our rainbow image, we would be living in perfect racial harmony.

(Cue: 'Ebony and Ivory' ...)

I find this lie fascinating. Racists, in reality, are among us. We *are* the racists. 'They' are not from another planet. But we dare not indict ourselves.

SKETCH FOUR:

I was an obsessive competitive debater throughout my university career. And so when I arrived at Oxford University I was naturally drawn to the famous Oxford Debate Union. Probably the best part of my Oxford experience was the time spent growing as a debater, interacting with world-famous politicians and newsmakers. The Union was a space that was so well respected that, frankly, it was a feather in the career cap of anyone – even a state president – to be asked to speak there. But make no mistake, you had to know your stuff, lest the ambitious young Oxford lions, invariably wearing black tie, would offer you a lethal point of information or, worse, deliver paper speeches from the floor, that crushed your evidence or your reasoning. Fun stuff. Challenging stuff.

And so, in my first term at Oxford, I joined the Union and attended as many of the events as possible. During one of my first attendances, I found myself sitting in the main chamber of the Union. I do not recall the topic, but it was magnificent stuff with good opening speeches from both sides. Then it was the turn of a black guy who had been invited to the event.

As the man got up and walked up to the podium, I found myself thinking, 'Pleeeeeease don't fuck this up! Pleeeease be the best speaker!'

The basis of my mixture of fear and hope was simply that he was black. When the other speakers spoke, I had zero feelings about how they might or should perform. Whether they excelled or sank was neither here nor there. I had no stake in how well they might do that night. And yet, this stranger induced in me –

purely because he was black – fear that he might not be up to the task at hand, and a simultaneous desire that he should deliver a speech worthy of a two-minute standing ovation.

Isn't it interesting that my racial affinity could do all this to me? Years later, I am not so sure if much has changed. I still, for example, find myself desperately wanting black debaters to beat white debaters in competition; not just because I happen to coach some of them, but because black excellence is far closer to my heart than white excellence. It is a reality that is found in every part of my psyche. It is, for example, more important to me that Pieter De Villiers, former Springbok rugby coach, should have a brilliant record as coach than it is important to me that one Jake White should have a brilliant record as national coach. What is the basis of my split loyalties? Pieter looks and sounds more like my dad and me than Jake White. (Well, actually, *no-one* sounds like Pieterjie!) That's how deep racial identity runs in me.

These four stories are variations on a theme: our racial baggage, as a nation recovering from a deeply racist past, is massive. Yet the way we deal with that past, in the present, is not very healthy.

First, we are in denial about the fact that racial identities are still very strong, and that they often form the basis of racial prejudices, and irrational racial affinities. Many of us who acknowledge this reality pull a different trick. We pretend the problem is small. Or we pretend that we never were, and never will be, part of the problem. The problem is out there. It is not in *my* home, in *my* heart, in *my* headspace.

This is why the collective outrage against Jessica's racist tweet is slightly less comforting than it might appear at first glance. On the one hand, it is great that we collectively punish a racist in our midst. It means we do not tolerate racism rearing its divisive head. But there was, on the other hand, something disturbingly quick about the intense and voluminous reactions – something I am suspicious of.

My fear is that much of the outrage was less about Jessica's racism than about deflecting attention from our selves. No-one who came down hard on Jessica acknowledged their own racial baggage. The subtext of the criticism was clear, 'I am not Jessica. I am different.' And this is why my Facebook friend could so neatly distinguish between 'us' and 'them'. The 'us' refers to us innocent ones, and the 'them' refers to them racist bunch! But this is disingenuous.

The real difference, frankly, between Jessica and us is that she got busted and we did not. It is a little bit like our outrage when a famous person gets caught for drunken driving. It is easy to be outraged by that person's irresponsible behaviour. In reality, many thousands of South Africans drive over the legal limit every weekend and do not get stopped. Yet, with no hint of irony, these same offenders are often the first to throw stones in the direction of the busted one. It is a tactic that is aimed at drawing attention away from one's own behaviour. It is a lie we cannot afford to encourage in ourselves and in others.

The problem with pretending that we are oh-so-different from Jessica is unless we acknowledge the scope of the problem, we cannot deal with racism and racial baggage. That is why it is important that we examine our own lives, and not just preoccupy ourselves with spotting racism in others.

It is for the same reason that I introduced gentle disagreement into the braai conversation at my friend's house. I suggested that it was probably not true that Jessica grew up in a racist attic. But of course it is a wonderful fantasy. Since you and I live in amazingly progressive and cosmopolitan places, we never could have done what Jessica did, nor would we ever. After the attic, Jessica cannot handle the pristine multiracial space in which her modelling career has landed her. This is the logic underlying the other braai guest's casual suggestion that Jessica grew up in a closed community.

Again, we should be careful not to convince ourselves that racial baggage is a small problem out there. Jessica grew up in our communities. She is not one-of-a-kind. She is our friend, lover, sister, daughter and colleague. She is not an alien, and her birthplace is not Mars – it is in fact South Africa. She was born in 1992, and so cannot even be written off as a relic from Verwoerdian days. She is a proverbial 'born free' – but, not quite. Rather, born into racial baggage. Like all of us.

We dare not pretend our racial issues are over and done with, or negligible. Jessica is one of us.

It is also evident that besides racial prejudice, racial identity runs deeper than we like to believe. This is not even necessarily a poisonous truth and yet we deny it. There is no inherent harm in my quiet desire to see black debaters excel. In fact, given the historic educational inequities that partly explain why no black African has won the South African National Debate Championship (at the time of writing this book), one might even say that my passion for disproportionately focusing my coaching energy on black debaters, is sensible. Yet how many of us would own up to be motivated by race in this fairly innocuous sense? Few of us, because we have closed the space in which we can be open about our racial identities.

My experience of the two brawling women in the Rosebank Mall parking lot is not exceptional. When I tested my story with many friends less 'race-obsessed' than me, a familiar smile ran across their faces – they recognised the story instantly. I got the same reaction to my tale about the black speaker at Oxford. There seems to be a kind of trope here that is unsurprising. If I grew up in a community that was predominantly black, and had my first real interracial contact, socially, at my former whites-only high school, then it isn't surprising that I should have racial loyalties. It would be more surprising if I did not.

Yet we run away from these realities. We pretend it is only Eusebius who sees race everywhere – him and his handful of race-obsessed friends. But, how many South Africans reading this essay do not have friends or lovers predominantly from the same racial group? How many people reading this essay grew up in racially integrated neighbourhoods? How many of us, unlike the old white landlady in Sandton, could comfortably live with people who do not look like us? We have tighter social bonds with people of our own racial make-up than those who do not share the randomness of skin colour.

The story of multiracial, rainbow nation bliss is grossly exaggerated. We are not there, and we will take longer to get there if we convince ourselves that we have already arrived. We haven't. If someone like my friend Seth didn't own up to the fact that he took my skin colour as an indication of whether or not I was competent, then how could Seth ever have confronted his own racial stereotyping? It is only by acknowledging, in the first instance, that the racial challenges start with our individual selves that we have a fighting chance of achieving that elusive non-racial South Africa we chant about more often than we bother to work at creating.

And this is why I am grateful that Jessica put up her racist hand and demanded our attention. In the end it is the Jessicas of this world who keep us brutally honest.

AM I BLACK OR AM I COLOURED?

WHAT FEELINGS DOES GROUP IDENTITY EVOKE IN US?

DOES THE FATE OF THE COLOURED COMMUNITY BEAR
TESTIMONY TO VERWOERD'S LEGACY?

CAPE TOWN'S DIRTY, COLOURED SECRETS

Last year I travelled to Cape Town and got out in Long Street. As soon as I was out of the taxi, two little midgets ran after me rather aggressively, 'Mister! Mister! Something, please?!' They looked about twenty, or perhaps slightly older, but with the bodies of eight-year-olds, and certainly not taller. They were incredibly persistent as they begged for money, running in front of me, blocking my path. They looked and behaved like feral animals. I felt a mix of emotions: anger, annoyance, sadness.

When I told the story about a year later to a liberal white guy (and someone who is rather passionate about defending Cape Town as a blissful haven for all), he was deeply offended by my use of the word 'feral'.

'How can you describe people as feral?!' he hissed. Such is the smugness and self-indulgence of many white liberal South Africans that I knew he would not understand my point. So I didn't bother trying to explain myself for more than a few seconds, and no doubt his respect for me – what little he had – vanished.

But I don't take back my words; nor do I regret the depth and strength of emotion that I felt as I negotiated the two aggressive beggars. I tried a number of tactics to escape their gaze, but none worked. I tried to pretend they were invisible, but they persisted in blocking my path. I pretended to be deaf, but their hand gestures took care of that: palms facing up, one on top of the other, like a Catholic waiting for Holy Communion (but without the dignified silence of a parishioner). I tried to be direct and firm – 'I don't have money, leave me alone please!' – but that was met with the unexpected observation, 'You's from JO-buuurg!' By then, I had reached the door of the hotel, and could hurry inside.

This is my regular experience of the coloured underclass in Cape Town. It is obvious to anyone who knows this city that foetal alcohol syndrome is rife. It doesn't help that many white farmers still pay coloured farmworkers with cheap wine, encouraging already high levels of alcoholism. This, combined with the toxic evil of drug addiction, and the scourge of *tik*, results in babies being born with crippling physical and mental weaknesses before they have even had a decent shot at life. And this is why those men who harassed me had the bodies of boys: life had dealt them a cruel hand.

It is not surprising that they were aggressive: the alternative is suicide; or wasting away in a corner, slowly. They chose aggression. In the process they come across, and behave, like animals. This is not their fault. They are victims of society, victims of coloured communities' fate on the South African landscape.

I wish it wasn't so. But it is. And my white liberal acquaintance can go to hell as far I am concerned. These are members of my community who live like this. Those two could have been my cousins from Eersterivier, a very impoverished neighbourhood in Cape Town where tourist buses do not go.

It is inconvenient for wealthy Capetonians to be confronted with the truth in naked, unmediated, brutal language. Yet what they miss is that I *feel* the fate of my cousins, siblings, uncles and aunts. I feel it, I live it, and I drown in the shame and sense of helplessness, and the desire to wake up with a magic wand with which to make it all go away.

But for the guy who was disgusted by my description, coloureds are objects for academic study; for him, only unemotive language will do. He humanises the *bergies* (beggars) of Cape Town with language. I choose language that bears witness to the stripping away of their humanity. And I make no apologies for jarring the cocktail-fuelled conversation which was interrupted by my story. For me, coloured people are not objects of study. I *am* coloured. I love the coloured community, and it hurts to see how they live in Cape Town. Cape Town is brutally honest.

Yes, it has a mountain to die for. Yes, it seems beautiful. Yes, it is 'chillaxed'. But that's exactly the problem: we believe the lies of brochures. It is not really pretty. The realities of Cape Town are actually pretty ugly. And that is why I hate it. But not because lies don't exist elsewhere. Jozi lies, too. It is easy to pretend that all there is to Jozi is Rosebank or Sandton or even bohemian Melville. But of course, like Cape Town, Jozi has dirty secrets that middle class people like to forget about when they rave about how integrated and cosmopolitan the place is. The dirty secrets of both Jozi and Cape Town are a stain on both cities' images, like mud on a kid's new white pants.

But I dislike Cape Town *more*. Not because I think it is worse than Jozi. That's a lie too: the rivalry of the two cities' passionate fans is silly. I personally like Cape Town less for the self-indulgent reason that its lies have personal consequences for me. Cape Town, you see, treats coloured people like dirt. And I cannot escape that fact as easily as I can in Jozi.

Try as hard as I might to call myself black, Verwoerd – the bloody bastard – had the final say.

I feel coloured in my heart of hearts. I feel fake when I describe myself as black. My black friends don't *really really* think of me as black. Calling myself black is more a middle class luxury, right up there with wearing a Biko shirt, being intellectual-cool, playing around with racial labels.

This brings me back to Cape Town's dirty secrets. In Cape Town, as soon as I land, I know that I am, and also feel, coloured. Coloured people are visible, as is their plight, in a way that is not the case in other big South African cities. This is not the end of the world, one might think, but the reason I cannot stomach that fact is because it forces me to deal with my coloured shame. Cape Town, unlike Jozi, keeps me honest. Too honest, and this hurts. It challenges me, makes me uneasy, and takes me into places deep inside that I do not want to be forced to go, at least not on racist Cape Town's terms. I want to 'go there' on my own terms, in my own time – but Cape Town does not give me this control. Cape Town is brutally honest, and that is why I hate it.

As with most emotions, it is difficult to get a full grip on the nature of shame. It is also difficult to know when it is appropriate to feel shame. So I'm not sure if it really is shame that I feel about being coloured, and in relation to the coloured community.

I know it is not merely embarrassment at the sight of people who look like me, who look like my relatives, and who share a history with me, as members of the group 'coloured'. You can be embarrassed about something without feeling implicated in the source of the embarrassment. Embarrassment is, for the most part, morally neutral. I can be embarrassed, for example, if I trip as I walk down the stairs of a restaurant. Embarrassment is not a cool emotion to feel, but it is fairly innocuous in the bigger scheme of life's journey. It can even be useful – the prospect of embarrassment can be an incentive for you to do the right thing to avoid feeling embarrassed.

My grappling with being coloured, and my emotional reaction to the underclass of coloured people in Cape Town, is – sadly – not mere embarrassment. Embarrassment is not strong enough to capture the depth of my anxiety, my grappling, my guilt – and more. *Shame* feels like the label that just about gets it right.

There are two reasons I feel shame. The first is shame-as-recognition: I experience shame in the moments I recognise that I am a member of this pitiful underclass. The second is shame-as-guilt: I feel ashamed of myself, morally, for feeling ashamed of being coloured, for wilfully doing nothing to change the fate of my community, and for not challenging and eradicating the basis of my shame.

When I see a drunken coloured guy being a nuisance along Long Street, I recognise in that moment that I could have been him if life had dealt the cards differently. It also reminds me of my own family. I grew up with many family members who struggled with alcoholism. Of course alcoholism comes in all kinds of racial packaging, and has no respect for income or class. But a white drunkard does not move me quite the way a coloured drunk does. Put bluntly, the sight of coloured drunks in Long Street is a sight that is simply all too real. I can imagine being them, and I am instantly reminded of my uncle Alfred who struggled for many years with alcoholism. I often had to endure the shame of his violence and drunkenness as he fought with my cousins when I got home from school. The shame was particularly strong when friends of mine came looking for me, and witnessed the spectacle. It is that kind of hidden memory that the coloured underclass of Cape Town instantly awakes in me when I set foot in the city. It forces me to relive truths about my past, and my present – truths that I usually get to interact with how and when I choose. Not so in Cape Town – it is a city that takes control of my relationship with memory.

For me, walking around Cape Town is like paging through a photo album that contains a collection of the most painful memories of an earlier life. And because that earlier life hasn't changed much – a trip to Eersterivier in Cape Town confirms that my relatives look and live as they did twenty years ago – I am ashamed of their poverty, their lack of mobility and their ignorant bliss. And it is of course not only my relatives' fates that haunt me when I see a drunken coloured stranger. It is also, more painfully, the fate of my sisters and cousins in Grahamstown where I grew up. That small town, tucked away in a hole just off the N2 that connects Port Elizabeth with East London, is a town as filled with as many lies as Cape Town or Jozi. It, too, has the veneer of integration and cosmopolitanism, in the form of Rhodes University, one of the best places in the country for a liberal arts education. Yet, cross the bridge that separates town from the coloured and black townships, and you get a taste of the deep scars left by apartheid – geographically, socially, materially, and psychologically. I feel deeply ashamed of the horrid conditions in which most members of my community, including my sisters and their children, are trapped, like hapless flies in a Venus flytrap.

I am overwhelmed by the emotional burden of surviving that space, of getting away. And the only form of escape is to bury my past in the memory banks, and to assuage pangs of guilt with measly remittances home, and a flood of regular sms messages, and the occasional phone call. The rest of that journey is between me and a diary or between me and a therapist – when middle class indulgence kicks in.

But when I walk down the streets of brutally cruel Cape Town, none of these crafty coping strategies have any chance of working in the face of aggressive *bergie* midgets taunting me, almost as if they were sent by an existential philosopher – or the Devil himself – to make me panic as I remember my family, my community ...

I have come to the realisation that part of my shame about my coloured identity is actually self-directed moral criticism. I have fallen short of my own moral expectations. I have dropped the moral ball. I have messed up in the sense of not showing enough empathy for the plight of my family and my community. Or, perhaps a little less harsh, my empathy has not translated into action with demonstrable outcomes.

When I see Cape Town *bergies*, I know in that moment that I have absconded.

The underclass of coloured people is not just a dirty little secret of Cape Town that is well managed so as not to spoil the experience of rich visitors. It is also a community of downtrodden, forgotten left-over pawns from apartheid's politicised racial battles. And it is a community whose history is my history. It is a community whose fate I feel personally. It is a community I have neglected. It is a community I care for, and yet a community of which I am also deeply ashamed. It is a community I wish I was disentangled from, and yet I also know that it is a community whose fate affects my emotional state.

No wonder I love to hate Cape Town ...

ARE GUILT OR SELF-PITY THE ONLY OPTIONS FOR
SOUTH AFRICAN WHITES?

SHOULD ALL WHITES CARRY THE RESPONSIBILITY FOR
REDRESSING APARTHEID'S WRONGS?

DOES WHITE SHAME JUSTIFY WHITE SILENCE?

I'VE EVEN
LEARNED XHOSA!

It was late 2011 and I was rather excited to attend a debate at the *Aardklop* Festival, an Afrikaans cultural shindig that was held in Potchefstroom. Most of my work is aired in the English media. And so this was a chance to speak to the readers of *Beeld*, *Huisgenoot* and *Rapport* as opposed to the English liberals and intelligentsia proudly reading their weekly edition of the *Mail & Guardian*. I was driven there by a very Afrikaans boy who had been sent to fetch me in Joburg (little conversation passed between us, me being too snobbishly lazy to fake interest, and him too uncomfortable, possibly too conscious of the fact that he was mangling his English grammar).

The topic of debate for that day was hot stuff in the Afrikaans press at the time as a result of a media conversation I had initiated about white people's place in the new South Africa – I had rehearsed the argument of a philosopher colleague who is based at Rhodes University, Samantha Vice, about why it is appropriate for whites to feel shame about our past. They should feel shame, she argued, because a central part of their being – their white identity – is implicated in the story of anti-black racism. It does not matter that some individual white people did not directly do wrong. Shame, for Samantha, could be appropriate even in cases where you did not directly do wrong but an aspect of who you are was implicated in the commission of wrong, or in sustaining the resulting system of unjust distribution of benefits. One could, for example, be ashamed of one's national identity because of the actions of the government, even though you were not directly responsible for whatever government actions triggered your shame. And so the mere fact that millions of whites benefited, and still benefit, from the system of apartheid, simply because they are white, makes it appropriate for them to feel shame. A white person misses the point if they hastily reply, 'Hey, it wasn't me who did wrong, it was Verwoerd!'

I'm not going to delve into all of the complexities of this position. Of course one can disagree with Samantha about whether or not her understanding of when it is appropriate to feel shame is correct. Many have intervened very thoughtfully on this issue. There are also issues of intergenerational justice here that are tough to resolve: by that I am referring to the age-old question of whether or not we inherit the moral sins of our parents. It is clear, however, that Samantha's position is a very provocative one.

You can just imagine the reaction that *Beeld* got when it carried my article in a supplement called *By* which comes out on a Saturday morning. I have little doubt that many Afrikaners nearly choked on their *Ouma rusks* when they woke up, fresh pots of home-brewed coffee in hand, to that morning's edition! (I hope at least everyone's favourite rugby team won that day.)

To add to the challenge for *Beeld's* readers, not only did Samantha suggest that they be ashamed of their white skins, she actually went a controversial step further. Whites should also, she thought, respond to that shame by humbly withdrawing from the public space and allowing blacks to be able, for the first time really, to be authors of their destiny, and authors of our country's destiny. Morally tainted white selves should not crowd that space. (The actual argument, which appeared both in a philosophy journal, and later in a series of excellent articles now archived online by the *Mail & Guardian*, was more sophisticated than this, but what I have outlined here is the driving intuition behind Samantha Vice's analysis.)

Reactions to my article in which I merely represented Vice's arguments as a tool for debate, astounded me. I have never been confronted with such raw emotion, passion, anger, agreement and disagreement on a topic on which I have written. If anyone ever tells you that we live in a country where race does not matter, they are lying. If someone ever tells you they are the exception to that race obsession rule, they are lying too. The difference between the constant race motif in the utterances of some of us, and the apparent racial silence of others who self-satisfyingly imagine themselves to be simply 'getting on with it', is that we all have different triggers that bring out our deep racial intuitions, differences, prejudices, fears – and hopes. Reaction to the article, and subsequent debate in both the Afrikaans press and in the *Mail & Guardian*, is ample proof of this. In terms of sheer volume, it was one of the biggest set of responses *Beeld*'s *By* ever had to an essay.

Steve Hofmeyr, an Afrikaans artist who was last cool in the eighties, said in response to the piece, 'To fall for this pathetic propaganda will be the greater lie.' Presumably the lesser lie is his embedded belief that whites did not really benefit unjustly; at any rate it was not clear which part of Samantha's complex position he was aiming his blunt argumentative arrow at, but the resistance to her sentiment was clear. Another reader pleaded, 'I am not guilty of anything. I voted "yes" in the referendum way back,' obviously referring to the referendum that resulted in a 'yes' vote for the reforms the Nationalist government was undertaking in the dying moments of apartheid. Again, the sheer unwillingness in this remark to even grapple – not a willingness to accept or agree, but merely to *grapple* – with Samantha's analysis, is astounding. It reflects the breathtaking arrogance of a white person to refuse to interrogate how they might have ended up, structurally, in a better place in life than the average black African they employ as a maid or a gardener.

Comments via sms submitted to *By* were filled with even greater range and depth of emotion: 'I would rather go on my knees in shame for my sins and beg for forgiveness than feel shame about my skin colour!' 'Samantha Vice must drown in her own shame.' 'People like [Samantha Vice] who crawl up the asses of black people are usually the worst racists!' 'I am 63 years old, grew up very poor, went to school barefoot, never had money for shoes and sometimes didn't have food … some of us have our own feelings about the past!'

The most venomous response, perhaps, was a reader's recommendation to Samantha that she commit suicide.

I also got a call from a man living in Cape Town, who sounded anxious, telling me he had read my article and desperately needed to talk to me about it at that precise moment. I did not know him from a bar of soap. I was too bewildered to ask how the hell he had managed to get hold of my cell phone number.

'I'm having lunch now, I can't talk. Can you call back later?'

'Mr McKaiser, I respect you and I just want you to hear me out. I won't take much time.'

'Uhm, can you rather email me then?'

'No, I have to speak to you. I have to tell you what I think.' This was bizarre. I decided to hear him out, and luckily my lunch companion, Sizwe, could see it was one of those situations that simply called for his patience.

'I have read your piece, Mr McKaiser, and I understand where you are coming from but … *we are NOT all like that!*' (The allusion to a famous Afrikaans novel, *Ons Is Nie Almal So Nie* [*We* are not all like that], grabbed me instantly, and unwittingly piqued my curiosity about the stranger. For all I know he might never even have heard of the author, Jeanne Goosen, let alone be familiar with the novel.)

'Okay. But you do accept that general truths about group experiences can hold even if you can find individual exceptions?'

I wasn't trying to seriously engage him, but he seemed desperate not just to be heard but to be acknowledged and be taken seriously. So I had to give him a sense that there was no dead air at the other end.

'I've even learned Xhosa!' he then told me. I seriously wanted to laugh, but I could not. I was feeling sorry for him, and at the same time proud of him – he was clearly trying to make sense of how to live in this country, and in his own clumsy way he was taking steps that he deems appropriate to get to understand 'the other'. And while learning an African language is of course an excellent start, the sheer desperation in his voice betrayed a lack of control over that journey; it was more a case of verbal and emotional overdrive.

'I even just stopped a black guy here in the mall and struck up a conversation with him.' At this point I felt it would be irresponsible of me to not give an honest reaction to his well-meaning, yet unhelpful, melodrama.

'Listen to me for a second, okay? I really like the fact that you called me. I appreciate that you are grappling with this issue and you are responding with an honesty that is sorely lacking in many white South Africans. But here is the irony my friend.

Think for a second of this question: is it possible for the average black guy to walk up to a white person in a mall and just strike up a conversation?'

Silence.

'I guess not,' he responded, with instant understanding. But I insisted on saying more now that I had him listening actively rather than getting stuff off his chest.

'So ironically enough, even your attempts to make amends and cross racial barriers prove, rather than undermine, what my colleague Samantha Vice has observed about white privilege. *You* can freely choose a mechanism or method for engaging blacks; *You* have the confidence of a white person who thinks the world owes him something and therefore you are entitled to be heard by a random black stranger. But a black person did not inherit such confidence, such a sense of entitlement. White privilege rears its head even in your attempted response to your own privilege. Do you get me?'

Longer silence, and then the question I dreaded.

'So what should I do?'

I wasn't there to prescribe to him how to live. He did the right thing to actively engage himself on these issues. All I wanted was to plant some critical thoughts, and leave it at that. Besides, I was being rude to Sizwe. So I extended an insincere invitation to the stranger at the other end of the line to call me again in a couple of weeks' time, promising that we could take the conversation further. He never called back.

I was recalling this as we pulled into Potchefstroom and I suddenly realised that I might find myself facing quite a hostile crowd. And they had home ground advantage – this was Potchefstroom, and an Afrikaner affair. What were the chances of a *verligte* ('enlightened') audience? Or, even more fantastical, what were the chances of a liberal Afrikaner audience? Surely slim to zero? I had given a few talks on the same subject in Johannesburg throughout the year, but it only struck me then that location can determine the tone, style and words you choose in presenting the same ideas. In a place like Wits University, where I am an associate at the Wits Centre for Ethics, the space feels like an extension of my home, and so I can happily engage an angry Afrikaner 'outsider' in that space. But now I was in Potchefstroom, and had no familiarity to bathe in.

Still, I felt a little better when I got to the venue and had a quick cup of coffee with the moderator, well-known television presenter Freek Robinson, and the other guest, a philosophy professor, Anton Van Niekerk, who had travelled from Stellenbosch. We seemed to get along well and agreed on how the event would be structured. I felt part of a team, not the lone, provocative, young, black upstart I thought I would appear as when the crowd was let loose on me.

But my comfort was to be short-lived. One of the organisers walked over to us to inform us that two bodyguards had been organised for the event, one to be positioned near the entrance of the venue, and the other closer to the stage where we would be sitting, so that he could react quickly in the event of an attack on us. I thought – *hoped* – she was joking until she pointed out the two burly men. Their earnest Rambo looks confirmed that she was dead serious – yip, this was not an intellectual game anymore! This stuff was existential; it mattered.

It turned out that the precautionary measure of hiring bodyguards was taken because Professor Van Niekerk had been assaulted in his office on Stellenbosch University campus by someone who had taken deep offence at an article he had written that was broadly sympathetic to the viewpoint of Samantha Vice. So it was sensible to provide protection for him. I pretended the protection was for both of us, so as to add a touch of drama to the story I would tell when I was back in Jozi (assuming I didn't end up in a local hospital first).

The next two hours of dialogue turned out to be absolutely amazing. There was no need for even half a bodyguard. Violence seemed as likely as the Pope admitting to secretly being an atheist. Questions and comments from the floor made it crystal clear to me that this crowd, consisting of folks mostly over 40 years, almost exclusively white and Afrikaans, and numbering about 100 or so, was a crowd that was *gatvol* ('sick and tired') of the dominant narrative about whites in the public space, especially within the Afrikaans media itself. And with each comment, each story, it dawned on me that I was right when I had written in the *Sunday Times* previously about the importance of whites reclaiming the public narrative about themselves.

In that *Sunday Times* article I had criticised what I regard as a false dichotomy when it comes to viewpoints by whites that are carried in the public space: either someone – call them Antjie Krog for argument's sake – is so consumed by regret and guilt that they are begging to be black; or they are so full of self-pity – call them Rian Malan – that they imagine themselves to be a resident alien in their native country courtesy of the perceived hostility of the natives. Where was the voice of a white person comfortable enough with her entitlement as a citizen to participate in public life, in the creation of a new society, and yet doing so with full awareness of the structural inequalities that persist and from which she had benefited? I refused to believe that most whites have a portrait of either Krog or Malan in their wallets. I suspected that, in reality, most whites hated the caricature of their nuanced relationships with the new South Africa. And here, in front of me, the anti-climax of a drama-free debate in this hall was traded for the excitement of witnessing an alternative narrative.

Ruda Landman, most famous for her years of anchoring the investigative television show *Carte Blanche*, was in the audience, with her husband JP Landman. Both of them made interventions that stuck with me. Ruda shared an uncomfortable experience she had had the previous evening, having attended another talk at the festival. She met someone who wanted to chat and all went well until the person cracked a crude racist joke. Ruda was shocked, and stunned into silence. She quickly ended the conversation. Yet, the incident bothered her. And she had been mulling over it the night before, and during the discussion unfolding. It wasn't only the naked racism that had shocked her, but something about her own reaction that didn't sit well with her.

'And I realise what bothered me: choosing silence. I should have spoken out. The moment required of me to not be complicit. Silence is not always enough. I should have done more.'

I found this profoundly reflective. It is not only the details of the incident that make me remember it, but more importantly it is the reflective self-awareness on Ruda's part that is important. While I disagree with Samantha Vice's suggestion that whites should humbly withdraw from the public sphere – they are citizens just like their black counterparts – I do think that being colour-blind and ahistorical in how we negotiate the world we have inherited from our racist past, is a tragedy. And so an admirable way of living with your white skin, which is tainted by its implication in the story of anti-black racism (Samantha is right about that much), is to live in reflective self-awareness of how racism still structures the world, and to make a contribution, on a micro-level, to speaking out – at the very least.

At the same time, Ruda was happy to be critical of what is not yet right in our society, and was comfortable about addressing what she regarded as failures on the part of a majority black government. This, for me, is exactly how whites should negotiate their identity in the new South Africa: do not feel guilty for being white. Rather, fully engage as an active citizen with democratic entitlements, and yet live with reflective self-awareness that your skin colour still represents massive social capital such that you are called upon to speak out against the perpetuation of white privilege and manifestations of racism. Silence and withdrawal (despite Samantha's well-meaning recommendation that whites do so) can actually turn out to be moral cowardice, as Ruda had rightly concluded the night before. In her story we have a third white way of being: an alternative to the self-flagellation of Krog and the self-pity of Malan.

The sentiments expressed by Ruda found resonance with other audience members, including her exuberant husband, JP Landman, well-known policy and trend analyst. There wasn't a hint of guilt or pity in his energetic engagement that day. He was – is – very comfortable in his skin. I recently called him, having a fading 32-year-old brain, to make sure I was accurately recalling his remarks, and again, within seconds, I could instantly feel his powerful thoughtfulness on this thorny identity issue.

'Eusebius, look, for me the question of privilege is simple. As whites we continue to benefit hugely, materially, from the results of apartheid. How can you not acknowledge that, and feel regret about it? Let me tell you an interesting statistic that I heard at a conference I attended yesterday. A comprehensive survey was done to test how different groups, segmented in the analysis across race and Living Standard Measurement brackets, feel about their lot in society compared with others. The question was something like, "Do you feel others live in the same circumstances as you, worse than yours or better?" The formulation was perhaps slightly different but that's the issue it was testing for.'

'That's interesting. What came out of it?'

'Some 46% of whites say that they believe other South Africans – of all races – enjoy the same quality of life as them!'

'Wow.'

'That is a confession of shocking ignorance or blatant racism,' he added.

Well put, and I could not agree with him more. The inability of many white South Africans to see blatant examples of gross inequalities and structural injustices everywhere, astounds me. And JP was expressing in very clear terms the kind of awareness that someone like writer Antjie Krog does, yes, also have. But there is a difference in his attitude towards his own whiteness. It is this: although he berates those white people who are simply ignorant of their unearned privileges, doing so does not make him lead a life that is overburdened by guilt. I tried to explore this a little further, to tease out this headspace that I have dubbed 'the third way'.

'I hear you JP but at the same time I wonder how you, personally, strike a balance between not being that ignorant as a white person but at the same not walking around wanting to beat yourself up because of your skin colour, like some English liberals sometimes appear to do. You get me?'

'I do, and that's a difficult one. I'd have to think about it … uhm, well, two important points here, Eusebius. First, I refuse to see myself as a victim. I am not a victim, I continue to benefit from the consequences of the previous unjust system. I think it is important, secondly, to have compassion. Compassion is a key part of the answer. If you cannot experience, as a white person, compassion for other South Africans then I cannot see how you can live here.'

I am so not religious but the 'Amens' that popped into my head during this conversation were too frequent to write down on paper. Compassion is a powerful idea. It forces you to get into someone else's headspace, and their heart – to understand the journey they have been through. There is not just arrogance at the heart of those sms messages in *Beeld* I mentioned earlier; there is also a profound, and sad, lack of compassion.

'That's spot-on. I get you. Fully.'

'But here is the thing,' said JP. 'You must also have compassion for yourself.'

I knew what he meant, I thought, and wished the conversation was beaming beyond two cell phones.

'JP, that is exactly correct, I think. Too many whites are too harsh on themselves! The desire to walk around and desperately make amends, to find black feet to wash, is guilt in overdrive. But it stems from not treating oneself gently – or what you call being compassionate with oneself.'

Krog is right to criticise other whites, but needs to be more compassionate with herself. Malan needs to be more critical of himself and other whites, and not abuse compassion for the self, for doing so will result in compassion collapsing into self-pity. That is the ultimate point.

'Yes, and it is not easy. It is a story of growth, and in my case I have a wife who is sensitive to these issues, who pulls me back, and I do the same with her, when we move beyond certain boundaries. It is about growing. But I am happy I did not emigrate. I tell you what – I sometimes meet friends who emigrated a long time ago and feel sad for their sakes when I realise they have not grown in their 25 years of absence.'

I don't know the Landmans. And I am sure they have many flaws, just on account of being human. Perhaps an enemy of theirs could find a black person they had maltreated or some other act contradicting what I am recounting about them here.

That, in the context of this essay, would be missing the point. Imagine, if necessary, that the Landmans I have talked about are fictional characters if that will prevent your being distracted by the real characters. It is the words, and attitudes, in this small set of conversations that bear out my idea of a 'third way' of being white.

It is not necessary to be shy to insist on your right to complain about the potholes, to march against a Bill that threatens the ideal of an open society, to call Talk Radio 702 and tell John Robbie your electricity bill was wrongly calculated for six months in a row. This is the stuff you are entitled to simply by virtue of your political rights. In fact, I would say they are your civic duties. Samantha Vice was wrong to suggest that whites should live humbly and withdraw from the public space and give blacks a chance, as it were. Whites should not feel less entitled to be active members of this society.

But there is a difference between actively participating with ignorance and without a sense of history or social justice, and actively participating in full awareness of the structural injustices that still persist, and knowing the historic origins of these injustices. Whites who are active citizens but who live without a sense of history and justice are shameful. They lack compassion. But whites who fully embrace their entitlement to be active citizens of the country, complete with citizen rights and responsibilities, *and* in reflective self-awareness of history's reach into the present, demonstrate that one can break out of the false choice of either debilitating guilt or disingenuous self-pity. More white South Africans should emulate the Landmans.

?

CAN YOU BE A RACIST IF YOU DON'T
HAVE ECONOMIC POWER?

DOES OUR UNDERSTANDING OF RACISM HAVE TO BE
ROOTED IN HISTORY?

ISN'T IT INSULTING TO SAY BLACKS CAN'T BE RACIST?

HEARD THE ONE ABOUT BLACKS WHO CAN'T BE RACIST...?!

It was at Rhodes University that I first heard that blacks can't be racist. An older dread-locked student, with a torturous habit of speaking painstakingly slowly (a habit I suspected was designed to win an argument by inducing a coma in an opponent), tried to convince me that blacks can't be racist. He failed.

Unfortunately, arguments can be popular even when they are not very good. Over the past two years I have *again* encountered people, this time around Joburg, who insist, 'Blacks can't be racist, dude!' It is necessary to expose all that is wrong with this absurd idea.

WHAT IS THE ARGUMENT FOR WHY BLACKS ALLEGEDLY CAN'T BE RACIST?

The argument goes something like this: you can only be racist if you have enough social, economic and political power to successfully mistreat other race groups. Blacks have for centuries been disempowered. They have not really improved their lot in life despite democracy's dawn. This means that blacks do not possess any real power. Therefore blacks can't be racist.

Crucially, people who push this argument often anticipate the retort that explains that we are now politically liberated as a society, but they say we should not be fooled by the appearance of political freedom: blacks remain disempowered in 2012 despite democracy's birth and Nelson Mandela's release from prison. Being able to vote in regular elections does not mean you have political power. And even if you have political power, you might not have sufficient economic and social power to be racist.

This argument is obviously based on the idea that racism must be understood – defined even – in relation to its history. Racism arose in South Africa in a particular socio-political, historical context. Racism did not, and does not, occur in an ahistorical vacuum. Our history is the history of how blacks, as a group, were psychologically and materially bruised and battered at every turn. Even though a black majority government now runs the country, millions of black South Africans continue to be socially, economically and, some would say even politically, marginalised. The new South Africa is certainly not an egalitarian society; it is anything but. It remains a deeply unjust place. This injustice means that the black majority are still disempowered. Consequently, they cannot be racist.

This argument, however, has a number of problems.

PROBLEM ONE: THE ARGUMENT FAILS BY ITS OWN STANDARD

The main claim in the argument, if you think about it carefully enough, is not *actually* that blacks can never be racist. It is also not that blacks are psychologically incapable of racism. Hopefully no-one would be silly enough to make *these* claims.

The real claim is this: unless and until blacks have sufficient economic, social and political power, they cannot, as yet, act in a racist manner. This position is actually not as radical as the people who advance it think it is. Basically the argument amounts to a conditional claim, 'Eusebius, I'm not saying you can't be racist ever dude! I'm just saying get yourself enough money, that stuff they call 'social capital', and yeah you're ready to be racist then!' But many black South Africans meet this standard. It is certainly not true, at the very least, that no black South African has this kind of power.

Tokyo Sexwale's kids, for example, could not plausibly claim to be economically, socially and politically disempowered. The same applies for thousands of black middle class children, and their professional, well-educated, creditworthy parents. And these numbers are not small. Most of the former whites-only schools are now largely black in terms of the demographics of the student bodies, and many of us who went through these schools are now middle class South Africans. It would be a massive stretch to claim that all of these black South Africans are so psychologically bruised that their apparent middle class status, confidence, upward mobility and social and political capital, mean nothing, for the purposes of deciding whether they meet the condition of 'being empowered'.

So at most what the argument should have concluded is this, '*Some* blacks can be racist; the majority cannot be racist ... for now.' But the proponents of this position do not seem to take seriously *their own criteria* for who can and cannot be racist in society. They seem hell-bent to simply push the slogan, 'Blacks can't be racist!' with no serious interest to examine what lurks beneath the claim.

The flip side of what I am saying is also difficult for proponents of this position to accept. Some whites are now so poor and disempowered that presumably they cannot be racist. I remember in the mid-nineties visiting my dad in Port Elizabeth – I lived in Grahamstown with my grandparents. My dad lived

in an area in Port Elizabeth called Kensington. It is not as posh
as suburbs by that name in big cities! Far from it; it used to be
the dumping ground of poor whites. And for the first time, as a
school kid, I saw dirt poor white people who looked like some
of the Afrikaners from my history textbook in chapters about
concentration camps courtesy of the Anglo-Boer War (before
post-apartheid textbooks renamed it the South African War in
recognition of the fact that blacks, too, were involved.)

It was a shock to my system to see white beggars whenever I
went to the local shop. I could not believe a white person could
look so dejected. The sight was unnatural to me. Only blacks, I
thought as a kid, should be beggars. And in a weird way I found
myself feeling sorrier for these white beggars than the black ones
– the sight was just too new, too unnatural for my young eyes.

There is no way – *no way* – many of the white kids and
their parents in my dad's neighbourhood could be said to be
empowered. They are socially, economically and politically down
and out. For sure, some still think they are superior to blacks. I
am under no illusion that poverty necessarily humbles one. Many
poor whites still harbour attitudes of superiority. But I also got to
see enough white men and women who treated my dad as their
superior – he had a great job, his wife was a professional, and he
was middle class compared with them. They dropped their heads
in his presence in the way my grandfather would have done in the
presence of *their* parents. And so the question is, if one can only
be racist if you have the right amount of power, do we concede
that these whites are incapable of racism, just like their black
counterparts? I suspect many who think blacks can't be racist
would resist me here, but only because they are not interested in
being consistent and principled in their moral reasoning.

PROBLEM TWO: THE ARGUMENT IS AN INSULT TO BLACKS RATHER THAN A COMPLIMENT

I often wonder if those who think that blacks can't be racist ever stop and think about the implications of this viewpoint for black people. I would guess that their chief concern is enjoying a kind of rebellious delight in the reactions of, especially whites to the claim that blacks can't be racist.

Yet, if one thinks about it, quite apart from robbing a white person of the entitlement to be a victim of anti-white racism, the idea that blacks can't be racist is an insult to black people. It is dehumanising. The reason is simple. Being able to do wrong is part of what it means to be human. If someone cannot do wrong, they are less human than the rest of us. Just imagine, for example, that you were born without the ability to ever think badly about any other person. That would not be an achievement, surely? It would be like being born with blue or brown eyes – luck of the draw, rather than an achievement. So you're not doing blacks a favour by saying they cannot act in a racist manner towards other race groups.

The real achievement in life is choosing not to harm others. So this idea that blacks can't be racist in effect diminishes the full set of human experiences blacks might have, including doing wrong. This seems to me to be a pretty good reason to reject this argument.

PROBLEM THREE: THE DEFINITION OF RACISM WAS WRONG ALL ALONG

The only advantage of a definition of racism that is tied to the history of anti-black racism is that it forces us to never forget the material conditions in which people live that result in imbalanced power relations. Imbalances in power relations create a climate in which prejudicial actions on the basis of race linger (even if such power imbalances do not justify racism).

But it does not seem to me that we should therefore say that the historical trajectory of racism is the core of the definition of racism. The history of racism, and the definition of racism, is not the same thing. And I think people who want to define racism only in historic terms are simply not thinking clearly.

Sexism is an interesting cousin of racism. We know that most sexism is sexism against women, and perpetrated by men. But I don't think the fact that this is historically and empirically true means that we should define sexism as historical misogyny. Our definition needs to be broad enough to allow for the possibility of sexism against men and women, and also for the perpetrators to be men and women. We need a wider definition because women are not the only potential victims of sexism. And not only men are perpetrators. So why don't we simply define sexism as 'prejudice on the basis of sex'? Then we have a definition that makes it possible to say, 'She behaved in a sexist manner' and 'He was a victim of sexism.'

Obviously, it is historically and empirically true, still, that mostly women are victims of sexism, and mostly men are the culprits. But that is a separate issue, surely, from how we define sexism. So we need to separate the history of sexism from the definition of sexism.

I think the same goes for how we define racism. If we don't have a simple definition like 'racism is prejudicial behaviour against another person on the basis of their skin colour' then we will not be able to capture all acts of racism. When a white journalist was referred to as a 'white bitch' by a young black politician, she was surely the victim not just of his sexism, but also his racism. But if we define racism as something that only whites are capable of displaying, then we are not able to accommodate the fact this white journalist, on that occasion, clearly was a victim of anti-white racism. So I would prefer a simple and, yes, ahistorical, definition of racism as 'prejudicial behaviour against another person on the basis of their colour'.

This is totally compatible with the historical and empirical fact that most victims of racism have been black and most perpetrators have been white. But these historical and empirical questions should not be used as a basis for *defining* racism.

Here is why: it seems more straightforward and conceptually simpler to recognise that racism is about unjust or unfair discrimination in any context and at any time. Of course we can then tell the painful story of our own experiences in South Africa of anti-black racism, apartheid and colonialism. But it does not seem to me that this painful history, and the enormous amount of collective work we still need to do as a society, will be off our radars unless we have a definition of racism that is historical. We are all too aware of anti-black racism's history; we need not sacrifice definitional and conceptual clarity to keep historicism alive.

In addition, of course, my simpler definition has the advantage of avoiding the earlier mistakes: in my account of racism, both blacks and whites can be racists in any society, at any time and regardless of the material conditions of that society; and blacks and whites can, conversely, equally claim to be victims of racism. This seems intuitively correct to me. And none of this is a contestation of the historical reality that mostly blacks have been victims of institutional and interpersonal racism, and that a minority of whites can claim the same. But we must divorce a clear and philosophically attractive account of racism, from an account of the history of racism. For this reason, I would simply define racism as unfair or unjust discrimination on the basis of race.

It follows that blacks can be racist (too).

SHOULD AFFIRMATIVE ACTION APPOINTEES BE
EMBARRASSED?

IS AFFIRMATIVE ACTION MORALLY DEFENSIBLE?

DOES AFFIRMATIVE ACTION
UNDERMINE NON-RACIALISM?

AFFIRMATIVE ACTION: A FORCE FOR GOOD OR RACISM'S FRIEND?

I've never once given a talk on race, or been part of a panel discussion about race, and not had to field a question about affirmative action. And on every single occasion the person asking the question is filled with passion, often barely holding back on very strong emotion so as not to ruin the atmosphere perhaps, especially in university settings. Recently, for example, I gave a talk on race at Stellenbosch University. And, you bettcha, the same thing happened.

I absolutely loved the whole Stellenbosch experience, though. It was the first time I had given a talk in a cinema (on campus), complete with a guitarist doing his thing, and singing gently, as students and staff made their way inside. This being Stellenbosch, there was a pub right on site, and truth be told I was wonderfully tipsy before I even started talking. It made for an honest, flowing discussion, and the students, I suspect, appreciated my combination of engagement, and the fact that I was visibly sipping the Hunter's Dry one of them had bought me.

I shared a lot of personal stories to make the point that we have racial baggage that we needlessly fear talking about. (In fact, my anecdotes and comment were based on another essay in this collection, 'Racial baggage in four part harmony'.) I could see the students were relieved by my frank, personal style and tone. Universities can be rather sterile places, with emotion reserved for the drama department. So they quickly warmed to my newfound Jonathan 'let's talk, folks!' Jansen style. (Jansen, rector of the University of the Free State, is a public intellectual well known for his ability to speak the truth – or his truth – powerfully, but plainly.)

They asked questions and made comments straight from the heart, taking their cue from me. I was very pleased. We will never make progress in dealing with racial – and other – tensions if we cannot learn to speak frankly. We too often fear that frankness must lead to anger, and alienating ourselves from each other.

This talk gave me hope that younger South Africans can learn to speak openly to one another, but with empathy, and with a willingness to listen, to be persuaded, and to examine their own deeply held beliefs and desires. Academic discourse, sadly, does not normally allow for that sort of engagement. Which is why, in part, I refuse to be a full-time academic, and rather try to bridge a gap between my academic instincts, and my commitment to public debate.

And so it was in this spirit of frankness that a white, Afrikaans student posed a question long into the session. It was clear he had listened carefully, since he perfectly summarised in beautiful Afrikaans the nuances of my viewpoint. I appreciated that. But it was clear he had a very strong counterview that was about to be shared.

Do we not, he asked me, merely reinforce the worst of apartheid's destructive racial constructions with policies in the new South Africa that still crudely distinguish between different racial groups? Did we not choose democracy over apartheid precisely because we wanted to escape racial categories? Why, then, do we have policies that are couched in the language of which apartheid's architects would have fully approved? Should we not, as democrats, know better?

He didn't share a personal story, but the controlled tension in his voice gave a clear sense that he saw himself as a young South African who only happened to be white, and who was committed to the non-racial ideal that our new society is based on, but who found himself routinely labelled a *white* South African rather than simply a South African. Worse, he could not guarantee that his white skin might count against him when he applied for a place at a medical school, or for a job.

It was a difficult cluster of questions, and I could only sketch him the outline of a full answer. The full answer, of course, is what I want to give in this essay. The challenge from the student can be crisply formulated: is affirmative action even in *principle* okay?

I want to engage with some of the biggest worries opponents of affirmative action have, and so give a sense of why, despite empathising with the logic and emotional distress of that Stellenbosch student, I think affirmative action is justified.

'AFFIRMATIVE ACTION IS RACIST'

I often encounter the claim that affirmative action is racist. The logic is that affirmative action discriminates against whites by excluding them from certain positions based solely on the colour of their skin. Job advertisements, for example, might say or imply things along the lines of, 'Affirmative action candidates will be preferentially considered.' Is this racist? No. Here's why.

First, I can certainly see why some people might be tempted to see these policies as racist. It makes sense, doesn't it, that if I say, 'You guys are equally good for this job but I'm going to give it to Sipho rather than to Freek because Sipho is black', you will think I am discriminating against Freek on the basis of his skin colour.

And you'd be right – that is discrimination. Many supporters of affirmative action would not admit it is discrimination. But it is. I have no doubt that at least some jobs that I have got in the past have been on this basis, even in cases where my qualifications might have been decent. In South Africa, for example, there are very few black philosophy lecturers. And if I had to apply for a philosophy teaching job, and another candidate was white but not much better than me in terms of qualifications, most universities would choose me in that case just because I am black. That is racial discrimination. The Stellenbosch student is spot-on.

But here's the thing: racial discrimination is not always legally or morally wrong. This is why it is short-sighted for a white parent to simply cite an example of their son losing out on a job application and think they have indicted the new South Africa as a racist, anti-white den. Not so. Discrimination can, actually, be morally and legally justified. And that is something that is missed in the emotional, and very personal, reactions of South Africans to the affirmative action debate. Few are even capable of listening to my claim that discrimination can be justified. They might drop their mug of coffee and Marie biscuit while reading this paragraph and dismiss its contents outright. (Sadly, critical dialogue can be hamstrung by strong emotion.) Let me explain then how discrimination can be legally and morally acceptable.

If discrimination is *rational* then it is acceptable. The oldest example in the book, of course, is that we discriminate against blind people. We don't allow them to drive cars on our roads. But we allow people who can see to drive (provided they pass a driver's test). But the discrimination against blind people is rational. It is rational because the ability to see is relevant to driving. If you cannot see, you cannot drive accurately and safely. So this is an example of fair discrimination. So the question one must ask is not, 'Does affirmative action discriminate against whites?' Of course it does! The real question to ask is, 'Is it *fair* that affirmative action discriminates against whites?' The answer is 'yes'.

When two adults apply for a job, they bring history and personal narrative to bear on that job application. History has resulted in disproportionate opportunities for development and upward mobility, distributed, deliberately and structurally, across race and gender lines in South Africa. Our history over the last few centuries, and which reached a climax in the middle and late twentieth century, is a history of fierce, unfair discrimination. Jobs were routinely reserved for race groups, with the best being reserved for whites. Government spending on citizens disproportionately benefited white over non-white communities. Particularly insulting was the education system: more was spent by the state on a white child's education than a black child.

One paragraph could never capture the full story of apartheid's injustice. Yet the number of South Africans who debate affirmative action in an ahistorical vacuum continue to shock and disappoint me. The underlying sentiment is often that only natural ability and differences in work ethics explain the strengths and weaknesses of two candidates applying for a job. This is a bald-faced lie everywhere but particularly so here in South Africa. Two candidates do not appear at interviews for medical school or for a job from nowhere. They appear from life narratives that have shaped their current circumstances. Anyone who denies this is culpably forgetting history, callously ignoring its reach into the present.

And this is why affirmative action is rational, and morally acceptable. It is an attempt to correct past injustices that were inflicted on us specifically along racial lines. Those policies were designed in racial terms, and implemented in the language of race, with the apartheid government treating different race groups differently. And since the purpose of affirmative action is fair – to reverse the immorality that has resulted from that racist ideology – the discrimination against whites which comes with affirmative action policies, is justified too. Just as the discrimination against blind people is rational, so discrimination against whites in the form of affirmative action is rational also because it is necessary in order to achieve a more economically and socially just South Africa.

'That's ridiculous!' I have heard many people say. And, trust me, I have heard the full gamut of objections. I cannot rehearse them all here. But one of the objections that irritates me most is the idea that we could not possibly know when to stop implementing affirmative action. This is an exaggerated worry.

We have a rough idea of what a just society looks like. A just South Africa is not one in which there is a perfect match between the country's demographics, and the demographics of the workplace, Parliament, sports teams, etc. That kind of numerically exact demographic representation would be the worst kind of deliberate design. Those kinds of projects are often rightly lampooned as 'racial bean-counting', but fears about such bean-counting are grossly exaggerated. Clearly, if 10% of accountants are black, we have a structural problem. If 65% are black, we have less of a problem. Similarly, if only 3%, for argument sake, of all A-rated scientists are women, then we have an unjust situation. This does not mean that 53% or so of all A-rated scientists must be female, but the injustice would be obvious if the figure was 3%.

And that is the point: in order to reverse obviously unjust situations like the hypothetical (or perhaps all too real) ones sketched here, it might well be the case that whites (or men) will not be treated the same as other groups. But this is justified because the reason is acceptable. The reason would be to achieve a *more just* society. In practice, this might mean giving more bursaries to black African students, say, than any other group, deliberately – or it might mean special research grants specifically for female scientists. These kinds of interventions do not undermine the idea of equality. They do the opposite: they take equality seriously enough to take account of how unequal starting points in life can skew fair competition between people. This therefore requires differential treatment in order to create, over time, a society that is genuinely egalitarian.

Anyone who says that affirmative action is racist simply does not get the meaning of substantive equality. Or they do not understand the connection between equality and justice. If they did, they'd abandon the objection instantly.

'AFFIRMATIVE ACTION UNDERMINES NON-RACIALISM'

Some people claim that if we want to achieve a non-racial South Africa, then we should not adopt affirmative action policies. The concern is that policies that differentiate between race groups reinforce differences between people. And if you reinforce the idea that race groups exist and differ from one another, you are less likely to ever achieve a non-racial South Africa. Is there any merit in this?

I struggle to see why these concerns are legitimate. I have never understood why racial differences should be inherently divisive. But let me grapple with the concerns of opponents of affirmative action.

I think one fear people have is that if we talk about race 'too much' we will stay in the racist past that we are trying to move away from. I often encounter this anxiety when I am on radio. Just the other day, for example, on Talk Radio 702 I was being interviewed about an open letter I had written to the editor of *City Press*, Ferial Haffajee. In the letter I had criticised her decision to take off the newspaper's website an image of a painting of the state president that showed, among other things, an artist's impression of the president's penis. I thought she had allowed political bullies to get the better of her. And I said so. But along the way I suggested that the editor's decision also undermined black people in a sense, even though her intentions and motives were to be sympathetic to a deep sense of disgust among supporters of the president.

I thought that she had inadvertently displayed low expectations of black readers of her newspaper, low expectations of black politicians, and low expectations of angry black supporters of the president. I thought she should have held her fellow black citizens to a higher intellectual standard – as she surely would a white group that objected to a similar image of one of their heroes. So she let blacks down in her very attempt to seem emotionally mature.

The radio talk show host was astounded that the editor could be accused of having undermined blacks, given she was trying to respect black people's feelings! Lo and behold, as *always* happens when this kind of discussion takes place, the very first caller predictably shouted, 'Why do we still refer to people's skin colour?! Why?!' They weren't interested in the real issue – whether I was fair in saying the editor had held blacks to a low standard of dialogue. The caller did what so many South Africans do – simply pleaded for us to stop talking about race.

That is not an isolated example. I could fill books with anecdotal examples. I once participated in a debate on Sakina Kamwendo's talk show on Metro FM talking about coloured identity. We actually called it 'The Great Coloured Debate'. And, you've guessed it, one of the very first callers shouted, 'Why are we referring to people as coloured in this day and age? My goodness!' It never occurred to them that not using the word 'coloured' wouldn't make my coloured sisters and brothers who live in homogenous, coloured, apartheid geographical spaces – still – from self-identifying as coloured. Linguistic denial can't make deeply-held, and very personal, racial identities disappear.

So we'd better get over our fear of the language of race, and talk. There is no reason why the language of race should logically lead to racism. I can recognise which of my friends are black, coloured or white without using that recognition as a reason to be racist. We should stop blaming racialism for our racism. It is a bit like blaming your sexism on the fact that you can see that women and men look different. Racism's the enemy. The language of race, and seeing differences in each other, is not the enemy.

'AFFIRMATIVE ACTION IS AN INSULT TO BLACK PEOPLE'

I remember once watching the exuberant Jonathan Jansen, rector of the University of the Free State, being interviewed on television and explaining with great enthusiasm to the host of the television show why he finds references to himself as 'black' an insult to the merit of his achievements. Being referred to as 'the first black dean', for example, diminished his hard work, and academic excellence, he argued. He widened the anecdote's reach to make the point that affirmative action, more generally, undermines the achievements of black people by creating the impression that blacks only need to meet lower standards than everyone else in order to be awarded accolades, jobs, etc. That, surely, is an insult to black people, and reinforces the idea that they can only do well if they are treated as handicapped and given special assistance that would not be given to other competitors. Is that really the message of affirmative action? I'm not convinced it is.

Of course it is possible that there are personal and emotional costs that come with affirmative action policies: one might – whether true or not – be recognised as, or assumed to be, an affirmative action candidate. This could result, yes, in negative stereotypes about one's skill-set, or gossip about whether or not one truly deserves a particular post.

The personal and social cost can be tough to bear. But how much weight should be attached to this in one's overall assessment of affirmative action policies?

We do not have decisive empirical evidence about how the majority of black South Africans feel about the design of race-based policies aimed at restoring past imbalances. So we are left guessing whether Jonathan Jansen's gripes are representative of the entire black population or whether they are isolated. After all, for every such example, I could cite a counter-example of someone who does not mind being an affirmative action appointee.

The reason I am fine with being labelled an affirmative action candidate is because I understand the justice argument for why the policy exists. If I had a problem with being an affirmative action beneficiary, that would be an indication that I had missed the point of the policy. Put it this way: when Jansen expresses deep annoyance at being thought of as an affirmative action appointment his annoyance is not a sign that he is a champion of black excellence. By being annoyed he is simply demonstrating that he has failed to grasp or to accept the justification for affirmative action in the first place. If you understand, accept and internalise the reasons for affirmative action – the goals of substantive equality and justice – then you ought not to be embarrassed at being an affirmative action appointment or being perceived to be one.

Consider this analogy. I am often gobsmacked by some of my friends who are genuinely hurt by perceptions that they are gay. At least one of my friends now practically introduces himself as 'not gay' in anticipation of the assumption that he is. Why is it such a big deal to be mistaken for being gay? Would someone mind being mistakenly thought of as the most attractive person on the planet or the smartest person in the room or the nicest guy ever? I suspect not. The only reasonable explanation is that being gay is not something the person wants to be mistaken for. But, if the person truly understands that there is nothing wrong with being gay, then they would stop having anxiety attacks about the mistaken identity. At the root of the discomfort is a failure to properly grasp that homosexuality is acceptable, and innocuous.

Similarly, anyone who truly understands the logic of affirmative action and who has taken that logic to heart should not be fazed by being teased for being an affirmative action candidate. This is not necessarily easy, I admit, and it can be tiresome to experience insults and venom. But it does seem to me that most people who are easily affected by these jibes believe in their heart of hearts that affirmative action is embarrassing. And *that* is the problem here: the failure to take seriously the compelling arguments in favour of affirmative action.

Affirmative action is not racist; it is not an obstacle to non-racialism and it is not an insult to black people. It is legally and morally justified, because it serves to achieve a substantively equal society, one that has redressed the racist structural consequences of apartheid.

sex

uality

IS IT WRONG TO DISCRIMINATE SEXUALLY?

DO THE ORIGINS OF OUR SEXUAL
TASTES REALLY MATTER?

WHEN IT COMES TO SEX, DOES MORALITY MATTER?

NOT FAT ENOUGH

I enjoy people's reactions when I tell them I only date black men. Some are shocked – 'What's wrong with white men?!' Others use it to explain my relationship status – 'No wonder you're single!' And when I explain that I am only *slightly* joking – I've actually kissed a white man or two before but the vast majority of men who arouse me and whom I have dated is black – people still shake their heads disapprovingly. But is it wrong to have exclusive sexual preferences?

In South Africa, of course, any talk about race-based preferences immediately raises concerns about racism. I'm sure that if I were to say, 'I want the father of my future adopted children to be taller than me!' I would at most get a chuckle or three, but certainly not a scolding or advice to reconsider short men. So what's going on here? Should I be ashamed of my preference for black men? I don't think so. I don't believe that one has a duty to consider everyone as a potential sexual or romantic partner, be it on the basis of race or any other characteristic. And I am happy to be consistent: I'm annoyingly aware that the category 'beer *boep*' disqualifies me from the loving arms of many body-obsessed men on the gay scene – but I defend their entitlement to discriminate against my *boep*.

Sexual freedom should be just that: if I only ever want to sleep with, and date or marry, people who are left-handed, then that is perfectly fine. It doesn't matter whether doing so says something awful about 'my past'. The fact that the origins of my sexual preferences are embarrassing or even morally indecent doesn't mean I should change them as an adult. We can regret the origins, but remain entitled to keep the preference. A couple of examples from my own life are helpful in setting up the issues.

A couple of years ago while living in England I fell in love. I had met an absolutely gorgeous black German man of Eritrean heritage. Never before did poor English grammar, delivered in horribly staccato German tone, sound so sexy. I would meet up with him as often as I could – call him Jonathan. I am not sure what the glue in our relationship was, since we had little in common, really, beyond being gay and just fancying each other. Yet, somehow, conversation flowed till the early hours of the morning.

But our sex life was lacking, and that bothered me. He seemed to hold back, as if he got bloody great conversation out of me about his life, his family and some of the issues that bothered him back in Germany, but in return I did not get what I wanted – which was to be his, fully and completely, including sexually.

So one night, as we were lying in bed in his flat somewhere in South West London, having just returned from another night of clubbing in central London at Heaven, one of the biggest gay clubs in Europe, I decided to have an overdue conversation, which I had held off on for fear of losing him.

'Jonathan, uhmm … I've been wanting to talk about us for a while now.'

'What's wrong?' he responded in his disarmingly bad English, which almost made me stop the awkwardness right there and then! But I knew I had to have the conversation then, or never.

'I really like you. But we never have sex. Are you really attracted to me?'

'Ja. I like you. Much.' He responded, sheepishly. I wished at that point that I knew how to speak bloody German!

'So ... what's the problem? We are never intimate!'

Pause.

'There is something I need to tell you.'

Finally! I had no idea what he wanted to say. If this had been in South Africa, I thought to myself with shameful stereotyping, perhaps it would be a confession that he was HIV-positive and he wanted to first tell me before we have a sexual relationship. But I doubted that was what was coming.

'You are not, how does one say in English, you are not really my type?' Thank God his English was too poor to hide his feelings. Yet at the same time I was in instant shock – deep disappointment.

'What do you mean?' I dared to ask that self-destructive question, instead of just letting it go.

'You don't have the body that I like.' I wish the recollection was inaccurate but that is a conversation that will forever be with me! I knew I was a little bit overweight and that he was an athlete with a lovely body but to diss me just like that! I mean ... I could go to the gym, if that was what it would take to be with him. How difficult could it be, right, to get a six pack?

Then he revealed what he really meant – and I could not have foreseen it in my wildest dreams.

'You're too slender. I like chubby men. Very chubby men.'

Silence. I was totally confused. He looked embarrassed and scared, as if he had just shared a deeply-held secret that he had told no-one other than his previous lovers. And then so much made sense to me.

'Okay. I don't know what to say.' We hugged each other for a little while, before falling asleep, the night's dancing having taken its toll.

Jonathan expanded upon his dramatic confession over the next few days as I exposed the depth of my disappointment. He showed me his porn collection, and I finally understood why he never wanted me near it. It contained pictures of morbidly obese naked men. By 'chubby' he didn't have in mind someone who is, say, 1,8 metres tall and weighs 110 kilograms. No, add another 50 kilograms at least. In one of his more comical pictures, he was in a Jacuzzi – his beautiful athletic body amidst those of five obese men. The occasion? A festival for chubby chasers (men who are sexually attracted to and look for chubby men on the gay scene) and chubby men.

I had to accept then that we would only ever be friends because his sexual taste was very specific, so much so that even my overweight body, for him, was as good as anorexic. When I told some of my friends about my disappointment, they shrugged him off as a weirdo, a kind of sexual freak.

But I think Jonathan's preference for obese men, black or white, sharpens a question that is needlessly reduced to race in a context like South Africa: should we ever criticise the sexual preferences and tastes that people have? Is there any point to criticising Jonathan's disinterest in men with fit or average bodies? Is there, by analogy, any point in criticising my disinterest, in general, in men who are not black? Or are these cases – mine, and Jonathan's – dissimilar?

I think these cases do have parallels. Jonathan shared an interesting story with me about his life, which explained how his sexual taste came about. Similarly, there is an interesting story that explains the origins of my taste. It is worth unpacking this a little.

First, one should always distinguish between two questions: 'Where does my taste come from?' and 'Should I change my taste?' The answer to the first question has no obvious implications for the second, even if it is tempting to connect them.

In Jonathan's case, for example, he had gone through therapy for a while because he felt that there was something perverted about his sexual preference, and this bothered him. He came, with the help of his therapist, to the conclusion that (unsurprisingly) early childhood experiences had probably caused his sexual preferences to be what they were. His dad, like many immigrant dads, was fierce when it came to pushing his children to exploit the opportunities of their adopted country, Germany. But Jonathan didn't live up to his father's expectations of him academically, unlike his other siblings. And so his dad constantly picked on him, belittled him and generally made him feel like the family embarrassment. It doesn't take a shrink to know what this does to the confidence and self-esteem of a kid.

In the school playground this was reinforced by the fact that Jonathan was quite a small boy for his age, and known to be not the sharpest tool in the box, a perfect recipe for being bullied. Jonathan told me that during these traumatic years, the only love, warmth and acceptance he had came from two friends who were also the victims of bullying. These two friends, it turns out, were obese, and were constantly teased about their weight. Though fit, Jonathan empathised with them as outcasts at school, and in their respective homes. Not only, however, did this become the basis of many years of friendship, but Jonathan grew into a teenager who associated friendship, loyalty, acceptance and intimacy with obesity.

When he started becoming sexually active, he was instantly drawn to men who reminded him of, and had similar physical traits as his close childhood friends with whom he had bonded as fellow victims of bullying. This is probably the psychological basis, he thinks, of his sexual preference as an adult.

But here's the crux: does this fairly random set of facts about his childhood mean that Jonathan must now try to change – to 'correct' – his preference, to whatever one might think of as 'normal' (and I have no clue what *that is*)? Surely not.

The only sensible question to ask then, which was my response to him when I finally got over the disappointment of not being chubby enough, was to suggest that he ask himself, 'As an adult, do I want to continue to be attracted only to obese men? Do I like this fact about me?' And, after some reflection, with a naughty smile, he confidently and sincerely said, 'Yes, I love big men! *Love them!*' That was a sensible response: the childhood origins of an adult's sexual preference are no reason, as far as I can see, to try to change one's sexual preferences once they become an adult. Only if you hate your adult preferences, perhaps because your sex life is negatively affected by the anxiety about being 'abnormal', should you be in therapy – or sitting on the couch with a best friend, drinking wine and strategising how to deal with the calamity. But if the only 'problem' is that your sexual taste stems from a rather colourful childhood, then there's no reason to beat yourself up about it.

I feel exactly the same about my preference for black men. Interestingly enough, my attraction to black men only started at university. Before then, I would never have thought of black men as potential sexual or romantic partners; as a teenager, they never entered my mind when I pondered over who was hot and who was not in my class at school. The origin of my inability to imagine being sexually intimate with black teenage boys, was the fact that I grew up in a deeply racist, working class coloured community in Grahamstown. Black men were people who either worked in our garden (for a pittance), or were 'the boys' that my dad managed in the army. And all the adults around me talked about them disparagingly. In fact, I quickly learned as a kid that the quickest way to insult my little sister, who was darker than the rest of us, was to tell her that she looked 'like a Bantu!' One of my uncles, in fact, was so dark that he got the insulting nickname, 'Kaffir!', which has stuck to this day. So as a kid I always thought of black men and women as gardeners and maids, and associated the worst stereotypes with them. In many ways, they – because we did think of black Africans in my community as 'they'– were regarded as less human than us. The quickest way to bring shame on your family, in our community, was to 'have sex with a Bantu!'

So when a good friend at university, Vanessa, wanted to set me up with a black American exchange student who was at Rhodes University for a while, I was shocked that she could imagine I might be interested.

Pretend that I had said, 'No, Vanessa, I find the thought of sex and even romance involving a black man truly disgusting!' Would my response have been immoral? We have, again, the dilemma here of needing to distinguish between the origins of sexual preferences, and whether or not one then needs to change those preferences as an adult if the origins are embarrassing, or even racist in this case.

I think that if I were to respond to Vanessa like that, then I probably would be revealing some deep-seated racist attitude towards black people. It is clear to me that my disinterest in black men, at that time, was a direct result of being immersed, as a kid, in coloured racism. Coloured racism in my family and in my community had clearly blocked me from being able to imagine sexual and romantic intimacy with black men. This is a great South African shame. But, it would be very odd, surely, to think that the racist origins of that sexual disinterest mean that I must go to therapy to help me see black men as sexy.

I have no doubt that the racist origins of that hypothetical response about black men disgusting me, would make many of us uncomfortable. It makes *me* uncomfortable. And I am ashamed of those kinds of immoral origins that underpin many of our preferences in life for all sorts of things. (Even Stoney ginger beer had a reputation of being a 'Bantu drink' in my neighbourhood.) But the key question is whether or not it is acceptable to say to Vanessa, 'V, I never, *ever* want to date or have sex with a black man. Only hook me up with coloured and white guys.'

I think that is okay. If not, then we would be implying that we should date without any discrimination. Why stop at your 'natural' sexual orientation? If excluding black men from a list of potential partners is wrong, on account of race, then surely I should also not exclude women, since that smacks of sexism?

Or, what if I do not have a preference for, say, someone who is disabled because of how we are socialised? We learn early on in life to pity disabled people, and this blocks us from easily imagining a disabled person as a potential sexual or romantic partner. But how many of us think that having no interest in a disabled person, sexually, means we should seek a post-hypnotic suggestion to change that? It seems quite clear to me that while we can say there is something immoral about the origins of never wanting to have sex with, say, black men, that it doesn't follow that I must now change my preferences as an adult. Our sexual choices are too personal to be given moral guidelines to follow.

The irony, of course, is that I eventually gave in to Vanessa's persuasion. So I went on a very reluctant date with Akel, a visiting student from Duke University in the United States, to the local Spur restaurant (of all bloody places). Within seconds I was infatuated. His charisma would have swept me off my feet if I had been standing. His humanity, his charm, his intelligence and piercingly innocent big eyes, drew me in.

Our second date, which involved a walk up to the 1820 Settlers Monument, ended with me stumbling along the pathway in the botanical gardens that connect the Rhodes campus with the monument on the hill, and Akel catching me just in time, staring into my eyes, and inducing mad love. Yes, I confess: it was cheesy, and straight out of a cheap chick flick. The rest is a Sweet Valley High novel (or chapter rather), interrupted by the fact that his life in town was inherently temporary – and he was a bit of a player so I could never really be his. Still, after Akel and I had a sexual and romantic dalliance, I never looked back: black men are now a permanent and sweet weakness!

But here's the moral of the story: the fact that I allowed myself to meet Akel does not vindicate any argument that we should change a sexual preference that has an immoral, irrational or psychologically dodgy, origin. Sure, with the benefit of hindsight, I can say it was a good thing that my childhood racism was eliminated in the end, insofar as that racism had stopped me from seeing black men as potential partners. But I tell this story also in support of the fact that there is randomness both in how our tastes are formed and randomness about how they are changed. The chance encounter with Akel led to a new world opening to me. Who knows? A chance encounter with a woman next week might close the chapter on a gay past, and open a heterosexual world I never knew I'd love even more than playing with men? It does not follow that I must hunt down a woman and test this possibility.

Random occurrences are just that – random. Sex, and sexual encounters, should not be engineered. Doing so, it seems to me, would be robbing sex of its rather basic place in our lives: playful;

93

in the moment; from the well of unreconstructed desire. Our bodies are the most intimate parts of who and what we are, and it would be unduly invasive to be required to have sex in the name of 'equality' or 'non-racialism' or 'multiculturalism'.

It is one thing – correctly so – to judge your white neighbour for being scared to share her house with a black man; but it is surely something else – wrongly so – to judge her for not wanting to share her vagina with that black man. Go forth and have random sex with gay and undemocratic abandon!

CAN YOU LIVE AUTHENTICALLY IF YOU ARE IN THE CLOSET?

IS IT OKAY TO BE OPENLY GAY WITH YOUR FRIENDS, BUT HIDE IT FROM YOUR FAMILY?

IS THE CLOSET ABOUT THEIR HOMOPHOBIA OR MY OWN?

'DON'T YOU JUST WANNA TRY, MY SON? WITH A WOMAN?'

In my second year of university I got a knock at my door in residence from another student living in Winchester House with me, a residence slightly off the main Rhodes University campus where I was to spend the first four years of university life. He informed me I had a telephone caller. I was half asleep, no doubt from another drunken student night out – that's what Rhodes University students, especially us liberal arts types, did. In a small town, drinking games are the chief entertainment, throughout the week. And let's face it: Grahamstown is not a sprawling metropolis. And so I made my way down the stairs to the res phone booth tucked away behind the bottom of the stairway, and facing the exit door from the residence. That was always slightly awkward because when another student entered through that door they could potentially hear your conversation, or see your body language. Neither of that was what I would have wanted that evening!

'Hi there. Eusebius speaking.'

'UB?! It's Daddy, boy.' Oh shit. My dad. My heart raced instantly. His tone was not good; he sounded shaken. And I knew why. A few days earlier I had written him a letter, and walked to the post office to post it. The letter was rather long – running to many pages, and, rather melodramatically, on about the second last page, it reached a climax with a sentence that few parents ever want to hear (or read): I am gay.

I had been waiting for a response, partly hoping it would never happen, and partly hoping it would just happen within seconds of the letter being posted, so that we could get the awkwardness, the rejection, the hurt, the discomfort ... all out of the way, please. And so I just froze, my dad at the other end of the line, clearly not in control of his emotions, and so not helping the situation. Thank God it was not a face-to-face meeting. I don't think I would have had the emotional strength to see his face, and his sense of helplessness that was so palpable simply in the words, 'UB?! It's Daddy, boy.'

My dad only refers to me as 'boy', even now, in one of two situations: either he is extremely proud of me – like when he sees me on television for the umpteenth time and states in a manly tone and with a straight face, 'You're doing well, my boy'; or when he has to initiate an awkward conversation – as in 'Boy, you and I must sit down and have a serious talk about some things.' That evening, it was clearly the more awkward use of 'boy' coming from the telephone line all the way from Port Elizabeth where he lives. I was glad he did not have the option of jumping in the car to come to chat; the distance afforded us the excuse of a telephone-mediated conversation.

'I just got your letter.'

'Okay.' What else was I to say? 'Discuss'?

'Are you sure, my child?' I could hear his voice shaking. I did not want to conjure up an image of my dad with a tear in his eye, but clearly he was not able to hold back any longer.

'Yes, Daddy, I am sure!' I snapped back at him. It was amazing. For many years now I have tried hard to make sense of my response. There was my dad trying to grapple with a new fact about his son – a big fact – and doing so with raw emotion, the stuff of humanity – and my response was to snap at him! I have still not settled on a satisfying take on my reaction. I guess one possibility is that I had had time to puzzle through all the usual social, moral and religious arguments about homosexuality being wrong and was convinced by none of them.

Consequently, I decided, before coming out of the proverbial closet, that I would never let someone's homophobia trump my entitlement to live an honest life as a gay man. I do not judge them necessarily: after all, such bigotry is often just handed down to us. But I certainly will not condone homophobia by giving someone the space to get used to me being me. The journey of grappling with homophobia cannot be at my expense. And this applies to friends, colleagues and family as much as it applies to strangers. I would not tolerate my friends, family and colleagues' racism, so why the hell would I tolerate and negotiate their homophobia? Something of this sentiment had taken root in my nineteen-year-old, undergraduate self. And I think – I think – that was the basis for my snapping at my dad; despite him meaning well in asking whether or not I was sure I was gay, I instantly resented what I saw as his resistance to the possibility.

'Are you sure it is not the friends you hang out with?'

'No, Daddy, all of my friends are straight!' I didn't really have gay friends at the time; at least none that I knew of. So it was actually true. I wasn't, as my poor dad was imagining, conscripted into a gay gang! Though, actually, Rhodes University would be the one South African campus where such rampant liberal enthusiasm could well manifest as a gay-drafting game. (If only that were true, though, in which case I might have been out and about in my first year already!)

'Are you sure?'

'Yes, Daddy!'

Silence. Then gentle weeping at the other end. I just wanted to hang up and run away. Instead I just stood there, in the closet phone booth (where my dad would have liked my sexual orientation to stay), and waited. For something. For anything to make the awkwardness go away. It was the longest silence I had ever endured in a telephone conversation.

'Do you want me to arrange for you to see someone when you next come down?' What? I could not believe my ears and I was too scared to confirm that my dad was seriously asking me whether or not a medical doctor or shrink or whoever else should 'see me', with the hope, no doubt, of correcting my sexual orientation. I was shocked, and politely declined.

'No, Dad, I am fine!'

More crying, and a final, 'We'll talk again, my boy.'

'Okay.'

And then we hung up.

I walked back up the stairs in a trance, entered my room and collapsed on the bed, filled with way too many contradictory feelings and thoughts to even join my dad in his crying. I simply buried my head in the bland university-issued pillows not knowing why I was smothering myself so tightly in them ...

I recall that story because I hope it gives a snapshot of the emotional angst that plays out between parent and child when one deals with homosexuality. It is also, however, a story that raises a difficult question: is there a need to ever come out of the closet?

The whole debate about 'coming out' is interesting. It often plays out in conversation with gay friends of mine, many of whom are not open about their sexuality at home, but who self-identify as gay. Many of them are also not openly gay at work. Let me be clear here: by 'openly gay' I do not mean that they do not go to a pride march. (In fact, many of them do, actually.) And I also do not mean to suggest that they are not gay activists. (I don't think there's an obligation to be a public role model or activist just because you are gay – though of course the fight against homophobia would certainly benefit in this country if more people in prominent positions in society lived openly as gay men and women.)

What I mean is that when asked by a family member, 'Xolani, are you gay?' Or, 'Are you sure you are not bisexual, John?' closeted gay people would not answer, unequivocally, 'Yes, I am gay.' Similarly at work they would not let slip that they are attracted to someone of the same sex. They are always on their guard, wearing different hats in different spaces. This does not mean outright lying; it can be a subtle game – so one of my friends, for example, working in finance, would not blatantly lie by creating an imaginary girlfriend (though many gay men do just that), but would rather be silent at work, pretending that sexuality is so amazingly private that he chooses to be asexual at work and, frankly, that all of us should too.

The truth of course is that if he was straight, he would be participating in sexual banter. Is there something wrong with this kind of closeted or semi-closeted attitude towards being gay?

I struggle with this issue. In the main I think that living openly as a gay person is a good thing. The justification I have heard very often for why someone might not do so is along the following lines, 'No-one comes out as straight! So why should I come out as gay?! There's no need to tell my dad just because you told yours!'

This is a blatant cop-out. The fact that this retort is often repeated does not make it convincing. When the dominant mode of being in society is heterosexual there is no need to come out as heterosexual because every aspect of life is premised on your heterosexual orientation. Heterosexuality is, sadly, normative in our society. And so the default assumption is that we are all heterosexual and that is a key part of our identity. If someone is actually straight, then they need not confirm that default assumption. They can simply live nonchalantly in acceptance of that social presumption. Simple.

But if that assumption is wrongly applied to you – for example, a colleague suggests your wives meet up – then the situation is obviously different. You, unlike your straight peer, face the prospect of having to deal with a clear misconception about a central aspect of your identity. However you respond to that misconception, it would be disingenuous to pretend that the nature of the situation you face is identical to that of heterosexual persons. It clearly is not.

There is a more convincing argument against my suggestion that we should live openly as gay people for which I have greater empathy, and this is the fear that one might be rejected by friends, family or colleagues. Often, actually, that is the real reason why some gay people are part-time gays who only let their hair down over the weekend, or late at night – after nine. It is the reason why many others do not even identify as gay or bisexual at all, and are permanently on the 'downlow'. It is easier, if you do not think you are homophobic or aiding and abetting homophobia around you, to pretend that you're not entirely 'out' merely as a matter of principle – 'Straight people don't come out of the closet so why must I?' In reality, things are more emotionally fraught than that, and are often about fears of rejection.

One young gay man, a friend of a friend, for example, experienced what can only be described as an assault on his dignity when he came out of the closet. His family, convinced that he was mistaken about his sexuality or the victim of witchcraft, took him to a sangoma who recommended the ritual slaughtering of a chicken. Bits of the bird's sexual organs were wrapped around his penis for a period of time. The aim was to rid him of his same-sex attraction. Needless to say this did not work. But the moral of the story is clear: irreparable family relationship damage can be experienced after coming out. The human rights of gay men and women can be sacrificed at the altar of irrational family and social prejudice. This kind of story is enough to make gay people, especially young teens, think twice about living openly.

It is human to fear such trauma, rejection and humiliation. It is also tempting, wrongly but understandably, to feel a sense of guilt that you are at the centre of the events that seem to be tearing the family apart – that is the kind of psychological barrier gay men and women, boys and girls, face every day. So why would one want to come out of the closet and let the family in on what they would regard as a painful, and even shameful, fact?

I must confess that in the face of such stories I struggle to be critical of those keeping their sexuality to themselves and a select few. How can I judge so easily? Principled arguments – any argument – seem grossly misplaced in the face of threats to someone's life, dignity or livelihood. It is this kind of sangoma-mediated assault on one's person that brings the question of whether or not one should come out of the closet into sharper focus. Well, should one come out in these challenging circumstances?

I still think living openly is important, barring a very small number of really dangerous cases. If someone's life is quite literally going to be in danger, then of course it is not in their self-interest to live openly. That goes without saying. There are countless cases, however, where individuals think the consequences of coming out will be more grave than they are. In cases where one has the option to live openly and the source of the discomfort can be handled, then it seems to me that it is worth living openly. For example, if your friends and family know that you are gay, and you have an established record, say, as an excellent businessperson, and the whole town, frankly, knows the badly kept secret about you, why suddenly get married? That is based, at best, on a hasty judgement about the consequences of being a businessperson who is known to be gay (and in the South African environment, barring very few sectors, being openly gay is not a serious threat to commercial and professional success).

A worse possible basis for dating women or marrying them is self-hatred. (And it goes without saying that one can of course be bisexual or even straight, having merely experimented with same-sex sex; I am not ruling out these theoretical possibilities but am speaking to countless men and women who might read this essay knowing their true sexual orientation to be gay.)

Each case, and each situation, of course, has to be assessed on its merits. And I have no doubt that in many situations the rational conclusion for a gay person will be that coming out to your family, or your friends or your colleagues is not advisable. Many young lesbians in South African townships surely can be excused for not living openly? The ones that do are truly brave.

But many men and women do not face threats to their safety or material well-being when confronted with the question of whether or not they should live openly. And there are two reasons why *they* should come out of the closet.

The first reason to live openly is, I guess, connected with my ethical convictions about what kinds of lives – homosexual or not – are ever worth living. And, leaving aside a full discussion of the age-old philosophical puzzle about what constitutes a meaningful life, one ingredient I consider central to a morally praiseworthy life is authenticity. Very roughly (and this imprecision will no doubt incur the wrath of philosophers), this basically means living a life in full awareness of your own most deeply-valued goals and projects. It also means embracing your freedom to pursue these goals and projects honestly, openly and with vigour. Examples need not be superhuman: a local musician freely stumbles upon a love of music, reflectively embraces the activity and pursues it with passion to achieve musical excellence.

An inauthentic life, by contrast, is a life with an excessive amount of self-deception and denial, either about what you truly desire and value, or about your freedom and capacity to pursue deeply-held goals and projects. An extreme example, for purposes of illustration, might be the life of a slave who exists merely as a means to someone else's ends, the ends chosen by the slave owner. A slave has no freedom, and often neither the space, energy and inclination to even reflect upon, let alone choose, 'deeply-valued goals and projects'.

It seems to me that someone who embraces such a basic fact about themselves as their sexuality is living more authentically than someone who is not embracing it fully and openly. And gay people in the closet display just that kind of inauthenticity.

Someone might insist that sexuality is not 'basic' to our identity or being. Some people simply convince themselves that sexuality can be de-emphasised. But there is self-deception of a grand kind going on here.

The tactic of denying the fundamental place of sexuality in human life is used to avoid the ethical dilemma over whether or not to defy homophobia and live openly. It is easier to feel comfortable with being in the closet if you do not think sexuality matters all that much. But of course anyone thinking this (with the possible exception of a truly asexual human being) is simply lying to themselves.

The second level of deception is more crafty. Because we do not literally find ourselves every minute of the day thinking about sex and sexuality, but instead pursue one thousand other issues ranging from the banality of a smoke break to negotiating the stress of a book manuscript deadline, some people take this as evidence that sex and sexuality are not as big a deal as a rampant gay activist would have us all believe. If sexuality mattered all that much, why does it not manifest more obviously, and more often, in my daily routine? Or so they might ask.

This is another disingenuous tactic aimed at justifying life in the closet. Eating, drinking and performing biological functions in the toilet are 'basic', and yet they do not preoccupy us every minute of the day. So the test of what is basic and important to our human nature cannot be reduced to quantifying the minutes of the day spent on that issue or activity. Sex and sexuality are central to what kind of creatures we are: they are the elements of our being that enable us to express love, to experience the deepest physical intimacy, to bond with a partner in the creation of offspring, or to simply induce a serotonin rush in a moment of sexual foreplay. Sexuality is a big deal.

And if sexuality is a big deal, then you are clearly sacrificing authenticity by living in the closet, because that kind of life is devoid of a full embrace of your most basic nature as a human being. Anyone with an interest in living authentically (and I would sincerely hope that every reflective person wants that) should therefore be overwhelmingly motivated to live openly and honestly.

How big, exactly, are the costs involved in living openly? What is at stake, really? Like I have already said, this is not an issue that can be resolved with a generic answer. Situations often differ. That much I again concede. What I would like to sketch, however, is an example of how many gay people often overestimate the degree of risk involved in coming out.

An ex-lover of mine (now affectionately known as my favourite mistake) is incredibly confident about his sexuality. I reckon he can rightly be described as openly gay. His friends and colleagues know that he is gay, and as my lover he happily met all of my friends, colleagues and family. He doesn't have a straight bone in him, doesn't desire to have one, and lives what seems like a pretty authentic life. Yet, he has always been convinced that he cannot share the fact that he is gay with his family. That is his last remaining frontier of sexual secrecy. The cost, he reasons, would be too great. He is convinced that his mom or grand mom might have a heart attack (for real). At the very least, he says, knowingly unleashing that amount of pain on his family is just plain wrong, considering that not telling them does not change the texture of an otherwise authentic life in the big city, Jozi. So why upset the delicate lives of innocent family back in the provinces, just because?

There is a coherent argument here, for sure, but it is an argument that is rooted, ultimately, not in the homophobia of my ex-lover's family, but in the self-hatred of my ex-lover. We often project the last vestiges of our own emotional discomfort onto others. In the end, we reason ourselves into the conclusion that we are protecting our families from the painful consequences of their bigotry.

Yet, it is actually often all about our own demons, if we dare to be honest. Our fear of allowing our families into our complex lives, into a part of our lives we are ashamed of, because we too are victims of the homophobia we grew up in (despite having same-sex romantic affairs that make us think otherwise) is so huge that we would rather park that conversation with mom or dad. But we should never confuse our own shame with unreconstructed homophobia on the part of our families.

And that was my sense of what was really going on between my ex and his family. Yes, his mom was not exactly a fag hag! In fact, she was disturbed when she figured out that I was probably her son's lover – this happened as a result of my penchant for sharing a bed with him, naked, in their house, which she discovered when she unexpectedly walked in one day to the ungodly sight of my semi-naked body on her son's bed (my ex was not home at the time so the evidence of our relationship was not conclusive, but it was very suggestive and she took it as affirmation of her worst suspicions). A confrontation, not helped by my assertiveness, ended the relationship between his mom and me.

Yet, even this story of a mother's shock and disappointment, is one that can be wrongly interpreted as evidence of just how much gay people are up against in coming out to their families. It is the kind of story that can be conveniently used as proof that mom does not have any capacity to ever be tolerant or empathetic when it comes to homosexuality. But this really is simply an exercise in confirmation bias: a case of looking for evidence left, right and centre to confirm something that we desperately wish to be true, 'My family is not ready!'

But having witnessed the full texture of the friendship between this mom and her son it was clear to me that the depth of her love for her son would transcend a coming out. There was a beautiful and stable rapport between them that I could not see being seriously undermined by him telling her that he was gay. I was, truth be told, sometimes jealous at the simple love between them. I remain convinced that my ex's decision to not tell his mom about him, and about us, was about his shame at being a gay son, and not her inability to negotiate short-term anger or even deep disappointment.

Of course, one might still ask, 'Okay. So maybe there was less to lose than this guy imagined … but what was to be gained?'

Lots. He valued family life, and family relationships, deeply. And if you value a relationship or a set of relationships deeply, then it seems pretty clear to me that those relationships ought to be based on honesty. This does not mean disclosing every single fact. But it does mean that you should be honest about central facts. And, given how basic and central sex and sexuality is to human life, having an entire secret life that your family is not a part of does not strike me as consistent with genuinely valuing family. My ex loved me; I loved him. We had a strong emotional bond, and at the time projected a life into the future together. How could he exclude his family from such a central nexus in his own, wider life? It is worth having faith in the love of your family: the result will be that you deepen those bonds, and set the foundation for a more authentic set of relationships between you and them. How can that not be worth aiming at? My own dad, and my relationship with him, is an example of precisely that.

My dad started out on a journey that evening when he called me in late 1998. It was painful hearing him cry. But I had to choose between being true to myself, and shielding him from dealing with his prejudices, and his sense of failure and disappointment that his boy child was not much of a 'man'. But I would have done my dad a disservice if I condemned him to a lifelong existence as a homophobe. More importantly, I would have done so at bigger cost to myself – living inauthentically.

My dad has come a long way. I am so proud of him, and what he has accomplished. Almost 14 years later, his love for me, and pride in what I do and have achieved, and his encouragement, are all as strong as ever. Most importantly, our relationship is more authentic, and more intimate.

Our relationship is also lighter, and more playful. He is happy to comment on my boyfriends, confessing after I had ended one relationship that he never really thought the dude was meant for me but did not want to disrespect my judgement; he gives advice on prospective lovers. He hugs me and kisses me as a grown-ass man when he picks me up at the airport – gestures of love and intimacy we never had before. He can call me, pour his heart out, and even cry more freely than that very first time; he can do these things because our relationship is built on love and respect. Of course there are still ups and down, but living my own life authentically resulted, over time, in him respecting and loving me more, not less, than before I came out to him.

Of course the journey wasn't easy for him. Let's be clear: he was not some liberal hippie, atheist parent who had travelled the world in a fit of middle class, multicultural ecstasy, and was now secretly hoping for a gay son! He came from a very conservative, Christian family and a community in which homosexuality was regarded as an abomination. So the challenge for my dad was as intense as it is for any parent resisting the thought of a child being gay. I remember one lonely, cold winter night when I was living in England and only a few years after coming out. He called me to catch up, to see how I was getting on. I had not been back to South Africa in about a year, and he was concerned. He then said to me in jest, 'I don't want you to come home one day with your wife and I am an old man!' and chuckled.

I instantly corrected him, 'Dad ... Remember the letter I sent you years ago? Nothing has changed.'

There was a silence pregnant with *déjà vu*. Some of the personal work he had done in the weeks and months after my coming out – speaking to his siblings about the 'issue', to friends, etc. – seemed to be coming undone. This time I could sense a greater emotional control than the first time we chatted about the issue. But at the same time there was still disappointment. Clearly he had hoped it was a phase. This is why many writers refer to a 'second coming out'. Often you have to come out twice to your parents, reminding them your sexuality is for real, not a phase like being a barefoot Rhodes University hippie studying drama.

'I am gay.'

Silence. Then, 'I am a man's man, my son ...'

It didn't occur to me that perhaps my dad was coming out to me! Ha! What he actually meant, of course, is that he had a conception of masculinity that did not allow him to imagine someone being a 'true man' yet sleeping, and forming romantic bonds, with other men. This was not about religion or culture in a broad sense. It was about what dad thought of manhood. That helped me to make sense of his prejudices. He was never really religious, and used to mock the Catholicism of my mother and her family. So now I knew that his homophobia was connected with a notion of manhood that excluded same-sex love. Homophobia comes in different guises, often grounded in religious text: not so for my dad for whom it was about his rugby-inspired idea of masculinity.

And yet, even so, even as I understood my dad in that moment, I dared not affirm his homophobia. It was his journey, and one not to be had at my expense! What came next shocked me further.

'Don't you just wanna to try, my son? With a woman?' With the benefit of hindsight, I should have laughed loud enough for my neighbours to complain.

'Don't you just want to try with men?' I heard myself actually retorting. He got the point and we soon hung up. And so his journey went – a few steps forward, one or two back, and a few more forward. Today, we are tighter than a newly wedded gay couple who had to wait decades for the marriage laws to change. I am glad I did not condone my dad's homophobia. I love him too much.

IS LOVE JUST A BIOCHEMICAL REACTION?

SHOULDN'T YOU BE INSULTED BY
UNCONDITIONAL LOVE?

IS UNCONDITIONAL LOVE EVEN POSSIBLE?

OH LOVE

I'd give my left kidney (which is still in very healthy shape) to relive the eighties again. If only pink legwarmers, bobby socks, oversized shoulder pads (take a bow, Joan Collins!), Afros (and Euros for whites), LPs and polka dots were still the rage! I must confess I had a wicked pair of sideburns until university, and whenever my hair was long enough as a kid (just before my dad – a warrant officer in the South African Defence Force – would insist on cropping it army style, complete with side parting) I would make it frizzy and play with my sisters' banana clips and Alice bands. Sadly, the eighties now only live on in the outdated programming content of the SABC such as that embarrassing perpetual rescreening of MacGyver's offensive mullet (mind you, at the risk of sounding like a confession-starved Catholic, I must also admit to having had one of those too, very briefly, in standard three). The official end of the eighties, though, must surely have been Whitney Houston's untimely death in 2012.

Remembering the eighties is a nostalgic trip to the heyday of cheese. More than anything else, I miss the music – thank God (if she exists) we did not lose Metro FM's Eddie Zondi and

– cue deep baritone – Wilson B Nkosi to the pseudo-DJs of the nineties who think that shouting rapid-fire at their microphones in poor imitation of black Americans is the way to connect with listeners. Mercifully, between these old timers' refusal to get off the airwaves, and Talk Radio 702's addictive Solid Gold classics, the eighties live on in musical glory.

I used to sit next to the wireless, listening to Radio Algoa while growing up in Grahamstown in the eighties. It's a memory that strikes me every time I think about that complicated creature called love. That was how I got to know the likes of Atlantic Starr and Tina Turner. To be fair, of course, it is not just eighties' music that obsesses about love. Love has been the staple food of lyricists for as long as music itself has existed. Even Motown classics from the sixties and seventies are knotted in twists of romance. I still wear one of those silly oh-let-me-pretend-to-be-soooo-in-love facial expressions whenever I listen to The Stylistics, absorbing their ludicrous literary comparisons aimed at making sense of that bloody agent, love! My favourite, of course, is 'The Miracle', which throws the following extended cheesy analogy at us: The sun belongs to the sky/The leaf belongs to the tree/The grape belongs to the vine/And you, you belong to me.

Ignoring the drunken possessiveness of this lyricist, the melody of this song has a vulnerability that reveals, in fact, the lover's longing for intimacy, a melody that softens the lyrics which otherwise threaten to own you! So, yes, love certainly preoccupied lyricists before the eighties. And of course love is, even today, the subject of ballads, rap, R&B, opera and even *boeremusiek*. Gosh, even hardcore rock stars like Aerosmith's Steven Tyler beautifully confesses, 'I could stay awake just to hear you breathing!'

And these days, of course, the hottest British music act is Adele, and here in South Africa, Zahara. Both artists tap into our yearning for solace; in Adele's case the confessions of lost love are even blunter: I heard that you're settled down/That you found a girl and you're married now/I heard that your dreams came true/Guess she gave you things I didn't give to you.

Melancholy is clearly profitable stuff. And it has won her enough Grammys to already secure a place in the annals of pop music history. How did she do it, besides having deliciously sweet vocals? She did it – to be fair to her, with a healthy portion of utter sincerity – by simply evoking in us our own, well, lifelong love affair with love, both lost and found. Love songs are definitely going nowhere. And so just as Panado will be on the shelves for as long as people have headaches, so the likes of Eddie Zondi will remain DJs for as long as love refuses to go out of fashion.

Yet, despite the enduring nature of love lyrics, there is something both sweet and comic about the honesty of eighties' lyrics that shamelessly parade our clumsy grappling with love. And that's why I am hooked on that bygone decade. Iconic examples from the eighties, on the not so small matter of love, are plentiful, but maybe the most iconic of them all are Tina Turner's hits which are really a musical recording of a painful autobiography filled with the travails of searching for, and losing, love and intimacy. Listening to her work is a good substitute for watching years of *Generations* and *The Bold and the Beautiful* or patiently trawling through collections of Sweet Valley High. And, unlike these other artistic genres, you get to sing along *loudly* as you clean the house or ignore irate drivers in the traffic. In 'What's Love Got to Do with It', for example, Tina rather philosophically suggests that love is 'a second-hand emotion' before rejecting it with the famous rhetorical line, 'Who needs a heart when a heart can be broken?"

Of course music is also fun, and one shouldn't try to rip the sheer joy out of listening to it, dancing to it, and having it play as we go about our daily lives. But, like all art forms, music tells us a lot about ourselves. The obsessive love lyrics are not random; they are a reflection of a basic human need – the desire for love, intimacy and affection. These are desires that transcend class, race, language, culture and national identities. It is a truly universal fact about us, right up there with the universal need for food and drink. But these lyrics from music that spans generations have in common the fact that they all, in various ways, highlight the sheer puzzle of love. We know that love makes us giddy, gives us a warm and fuzzy feeling, an extra proverbial spring in our step if we got it all that morning, but sometimes we can't help, being the curious bunch that we are, trying to make sense of the emotion, even if only to satisfy ourselves that love is, perhaps, the one emotion not open to much rational scrutiny. Or is it?

I don't know. But, like Tina Turner, I often wonder whether love is just a bloody biochemical reaction I have no control over, or whether it is as magical as the movies would have us believe.

And I do know that even as a kid, reading Shakespeare, and with no experience of romantic love at all, I wasn't happy with the assertion, 'Love is not love which alters when alteration finds' – well, why not? Is love supposed to be unconditional, so that when I no longer love someone, I should doubt whether I had ever truly loved them?

These are two big puzzles about love – What is love? Is it unconditional? – that still bug me. And they bug lyricists. But most of us – perhaps sensibly – just get on with the business of chasing love, I guess, rather than hitting the pause button when listening to these reflective tropes in popular music.

WHAT IS LOVE?

I don't think anyone ever answered Haddaway's screaming opening lyrics from 1993, 'What Is Love?' And it was a rather desperate, eardrum-piercing scream. But I don't blame him. It is an annoyingly difficult question. One possibility is that being in love really just is a brain state. It is no different from being on recreational drugs. If you pop an ecstasy tablet it changes your brain state and you get a rush that makes you feel a jolt of happiness. (I never took drugs of course. I think? Actually, I can't remember. Whatever happens at Rhodes – including classified memories – stays at Rhodes?) It is the kind of stuff that opens the 'doors of perception' and inspired much of the decadent sixties and psychedelic literary output from the likes of Aldous Huxley even earlier than the sixties' rush. But there is no scientific puzzle. It just is a biochemical reaction to the drug that you had popped. Of course, the feeling is awesome, on the sweat-filled dance floor with lots of other blissful bodies crammed around you like sardines in a tin, perhaps to the rhythmic dance beats of Faithless's 'Insomnia'. But, I'm afraid to say, the feeling is rather easy to explain – it's chemicals, stupid!

Love is no different. A nerdish researcher whose work I stumbled upon once and then deliberately tried to forget because of its ghastly conclusion – clearly he had no respect for our yearning to keep love a magical thing – confirmed that when we are madly in love the part of our brain that is activated is the same bit that is active when addicts self-destructively become, well, addicted to a substance. We really are biochemical machines, it would seem. And even though the feeling of being in love, or even just in lust, is awesome, it is a natural version of popping an ecstasy tablet. But, as with drugs, it can be explained scientifically. It is not metaphysical stuff, even if cartoonists draw stars in the eyes of their characters, instilling the lie in us from a very young age that love has amazing non-physical, divine properties. Not so, it seems.

But perhaps it does not matter that love is less mystical than the language of love would have us believe. Does it truly make a difference to the experience of love, and being in love, that a very clever scientist might be able to write out a complicated equation that explains the physical processes going on inside you as you fall in love? I don't think so. If I think of the lucky bastards I have been in love with over the years, and block out the nasty bits of our relationships, and indulge in the best of loving memories, it seems to me that the state of loving each other, and being in love, is what mattered. That is what made those experiences valuable. And because we are social creatures, we will always, I guess, court each other clumsily, bite our nails while waiting for a response to a text message, and nervously take a double glance in the mirror before setting out on a date. None of these social aspects of searching for love, and negotiating romance in a relationship, can ever be done away with just because being in love might turn out to be a big biochemical event. But I wonder how many folks would feel the magic carpet had been pulled from under their loving feet if they were told that being in love can be reduced to biochemical processes? Maybe we should not spoil their fun ...

IS LOVE UNCONDITIONAL?

As for Shakespeare putting insane pressure on himself to never let his love for a lover ever be shaken, that surely is madness. It is borne out of the romantic lie that true love is unconditional and can and should resist all obstacles that come its way. But is or should love ever be unconditional?

I think unconditional love is possible, for sure, but it is a very bad idea. It is often wrongly assumed to be the best kind of love, the gold standard of love. Nothing is supposed to be more affirming than the words, 'I love you unconditionally.' Sometimes it is said a little more romantically, not quite so straightforwardly, but with the intention of conveying the same lie: to quote Whitney Houston's hit song, 'I Will Always Love You!'

The problem with unconditional love is that it cheapens romance and intimacy. It cheapens love itself, frankly. Think about other things that we normally value deeply – literature, music, art, or even ordinary friendship.

I don't love JM Coetzee's literary output unconditionally. I love it for reasons that explain my literary love affair with Coetzee: his style of writing is unpretentious, and uncomplicated – simple register, no over-the-top character sketches, and an ability to let the narrative do the magic, rather than sculpting ostentatious sentences or phrases. (Of course Coetzee is in control of this technique, quite consciously perhaps, but there is still a clear reason I can state for my admiration.) This is why I hate some of the work produced by Coetzee in recent years, because the earlier literary technique – the reason for my love – has given way to some weird post-modern experiments. So I love and enjoy Coetzee's work, but not unconditionally. I might even say, more accurately, I love the earlier Coetzee but I don't love the later Coetzee.

The same, surely, goes for friendship. I don't love my friends unconditionally. I love them because they are emotionally mature and amazingly supportive of my follies and my trials and tribulations – folks I can call on when in need, when celebrating success or just when I need to talk rubbish and have a drink at Doppio in Rosebank. They have an amazing grasp of politics and pop psychology – leading to orgasmically satisfying dinner party disagreements about the state of local politics, or alternatively Dr Phil-like psychologising about each other, and about strangers entering our space. In other words, there are very clear reasons why they are my friends.

If I love them – as friends – unconditionally, then I would actually be cheapening those friendships, because it would mean that I do not care about holding them accountable, for example, when they fall short of the reasons that drew us to each other in the first place. Surely the reason – and duty, even – why you might get upset with a friend for not calling when you are ill, is precisely because you have expectations of each other – in other words, reasons (read: conditions) that are the basis of your friendship.

Obviously we are not so crass and transactional in our language about friendship. Or in our behaviour. But it is surely true, if we reflect quietly about friendship, that friendship is conditional, but it doesn't play out jarringly, transactionally.

Love is no different. I would be devastated if my lover could not give reasons to explain why he loves me, or why he is in love with me. If I overheard him say to a stranger, in response to the question, 'Why do you seem so in love? Think it is for real, and will last?', and my lover responded, 'Dude, I don't know why I love him. I just love him unconditionally man. I will love him whatever he does and whatever happens!' I would not be flattered. It is cheap romanticism. I would secretly hope that he could do better if pressed. The best kind of love is love that can be explained, where lovers have a profound awareness of why they love each other, even if they do not experience love in transactional terms in the hurly-burly of day-to-day life.

This doesn't mean we can't love someone unconditionally. Many of us do. But it is a horrible idea. It is that kind of conviction – that love is and should be unconditional – that (in part) leads to women sticking it out with bastards who cheat on them or beat them up. It is the same reason my mom took way too long to divorce my dad – she was raised to believe that true love is unconditional. It is a lie. Love and romance can be cool and fun, but should not be unconditional.

WHY ARE THERE SO MANY VIOLENT MEN
IN OUR SOCIETY?

WHAT DOES IT MEAN TO BE A 'MAN' LIVING IN A
GROSSLY UNEQUAL SOCIETY?

HOW DO WE ACHIEVE A SOCIETY IN WHICH MEN
AND BOYS ARE MORALLY DECENT?

OF MINI-SKIRTS, TAXI RANKS AND SEXIST PIGS

Why do South African men seem to hate women so much? Take our favourite friends, taxi drivers. Not only do they drive as if traffic rules are mere suggestions rather than laws to be obeyed, they are also stereotypes of the sexist pigs too many of us are. It is difficult to forget the footage taken of two young women near a Joburg taxi rank, wearing mini-skirts, and having a pack of men, as threatening as hyenas, advancing on them, ready to feed their lust. This happened in broad daylight, and without a hint of restraint. Fortunately, the women were not physically harmed, but their dignity as human beings, as women, was trampled on. I would hate to choose between physical and psychological scars. Apparently the mere fact of their gender, and their choice of clothing, as far as these men are concerned, justify sexual predation. Our society is saturated with misogyny.

The video clip of that event does not document an isolated incident. Some women have been assaulted for wearing mini-skirts. And all these incidents are just the tip of the sexist iceberg. Women get raped all the time, very often by husbands, brothers, dads and neighbours. The most horrific recent example is that of a Soweto teenager who had been gang-raped by seven boys and men. She had been held hostage by them, and they had the audacity to multiply her trauma several hundred times over by videotaping their cruelty, and proudly sending out the evidence of their deeds into the virtual world. The video went viral, and it was only after a local newspaper, the *Daily Sun*, reported on the incident that the girl was eventually found.

Tragically, she had been raped before, but nothing came of the incidents reported to the police. She was failed by her family, her community, the criminal justice system and, frankly, by all of us who sit in silence as we experience and watch the symptoms of misogyny all around us without speaking out and thinking through what we need to do in our own lives, within our families and communities, to address the underlying causes of this social malaise.

So why do we hate women so much?

It is important to distinguish between understanding why we do what we do, and excusing what we do. There is no excuse for violating another human being's dignity. None. Raping a woman is morally reprehensible. But we need to understand violent sexist behaviour in order to have a fighting chance of eliminating it.

There is little doubt in my mind that we are, as a society, still deeply scarred by the police state we lived under for many decades before democracy's dawn. Violence was the state's modus operandi in pursuit of its racist ideology. But violence was not only directed by the state in our direction as black South Africans. We also used violence in response to violence. It does not matter here whether the use of violence by anti-apartheid movements was morally or politically justified. The psychological truth of the matter is that state violence, and civilian violence, turned us into a deeply violent society. How could violence not have become part of our social tapestry? If you have seen, as I did as a little kid, someone being necklaced – the practice of putting a tyre around someone's neck, filling it with petrol and setting them alight, as punishment for allegedly colluding with the apartheid state – on a strip of green veld in a township visible from the back garden of our family house in Albany Road, Grahamstown, where I spent the first ten years of my life, how could you be unaffected by the grammar of violence in our society?

Violence became a normal tool to be used for expressing how you felt about someone, not just how you felt about the apartheid state. Violence had become normative. The idea of talking through differences – even in my home – was strange to me as a kid. I was more familiar with a fat *klap* from my mom over my head. Violence was – is – routine in our homes, not just on the streets where people were toyi-toying against state repression.

This is unsurprising. You cannot live in a violent state, and experience violence when you leave your home, and not show the scars of public violence when you go back inside your home. If you get abused at work, at shopping malls, at schools and universities, then of course you will show the symptoms of post-traumatic stress when you are back home. Even our schools were not safe spaces; it was not just our moms and dads, aunts and uncles, who brought back the grammar of violence from their hours spent in apartheid workplaces – our older brothers and sisters came back from school with lessons of violence imprinted on their hearts and minds. So is it really surprising that violence became part of our social fabric?

You cannot switch off your memory of violence as you can the flow of a running tap, with one small turn of the wrist. We were destined to become violent creatures turning on one another at home too – and, of course, at taxi ranks …

These are the structural and historical factors that explain, in part, why so many of us are sexist pigs. The violence we experienced affected our masculinity. We developed, and still have, violent masculinities. Our sense of what it means to be a 'real' man is informed by the overpowering use of violence all around us. We observe violence, and then roleplay being violent ourselves, in our sexual relations with one another, as much as in our more routine domestic interactions with one another. Our sexuality is not free of the negative consequences of growing up in violence.

Violent attitudes towards sex, sexuality and women became normal in our communities, in our households. And it affected not just the attitudes of the predators but also of their prey. Violence between my mom and my dad, for example, was such a normal part of their marriage that I did not think, as a child, of speaking out against my own experiences of violence. If my mom could put up with a black eye, then surely I was supposed to be man enough to put up with the pain of my older cousin raping me? I did not dare tell on him, nor did I even feel like a victim. In fact, I still do not feel like a victim of sexual abuse, and sexual assault. I feel like a liar when I think, let alone utter, the sentence, 'I am a rape victim.' The reason is not because I do not see the sexual violence for what it was. The reason is that domestic violence, including an older cousin raping his younger cousin, was – is – such a normal part of our violent social reality, that any sense of having been wronged seems melodramatic, and perhaps even unfair to my older cousin. That is how deeply scarred we are in our communities: victims feel alienated from their own victimhood; perpetrators, like the seven boys and men who raped the Sowetan teenager, feel confident enough to send proof of their cruelty out into the world. Why? Because they no doubt think they have an entitlement to possess such violent sexual instincts and to act on them.

There is a toxic post-democracy cocktail that is relevant too: the poverty-inequality-unemployment nexus. There are some obvious qualifications to be made, first. Sexual violence against women happens even in wealthy communities, and is not the exclusive domain of poor black men. It is also true, conversely, that many poor men and boys display perfectly healthy attitudes towards girls and women. But it is trends and patterns that matter; the bigger picture does, sadly, betray the reality that many of our brothers, dads and uncles are struggling to feel confident and secure as men, living in a sea of poverty and inequality that frustrates them, and makes them feel inadequate.

When you feel like you ought to put bread on the table, and society says you should put bread on the table, and you fail, you are bound to feel pathetic, dejected and frustrated. And, that is exactly the kind of outdated social messaging we preach about manhood – real men provide. Add to that message a context of poverty and inequality, and unhealthy masculinities lurk around the corner.

The most underrated poison in that cocktail is inequality. It is not, actually, poverty that is the most potent catalyst for violence. If poverty motivates gratuitous acts of violence, and breeds violent masculinities, why are so many countries on the African continent both less well off than South Africa and less violent also? The most dangerous poison is, in fact, inequality.

We talk about inequality so frequently that we have stopped understanding the word's meaning. This is particularly unfortunate given that inequality correlates more reliably with our violent behaviour than does poverty. We are one of the most unequal societies on earth. In practical terms, this amounts to a massive social disaster. If you have grown up in poverty with other poor boys in your community, and a couple of them are now driving BMWs in the suburbs, appearing in glossy magazines, or are in powerful positions within government or the private sector, you will feel like the loser who did not make it. Because the gap between the poor and the wealthy is bigger here than almost anywhere in the world, the sense of failure and underachievement our sons, brothers, dads, cousins and uncles feel, is worse than in a society that is less unequal.

If you walk a mere ten minutes from Alexandra, you cross the border into another world. You do not need to fly overseas to see London or New York, if you are a poor black man, jobless and frustrated, in Alexandra walk ten minutes and you are in a little London, or little New York, called 'Sandton'. Except here in Sandton you will not see many foreigners; you will see a handful of confident, healthy, wealthy black men who look like perfect versions of your poor self. How can you not hang your head in shame, store the shame and disappointment deep inside you, and vent when you get back to your shack when your daughter or wife appear in front of you like a taunting reminder that you're a failure?

Being a man in a time of gigantic inequality is not easy. And many millions of South African boys and men fail to respond healthily to their sense of despair, and deep disappointment, for not making it in the new South Africa.

I have no clue how we should respond to these underlying causes of violence against women and, as my own childhood story shows, violence against boys and other men too. We are not just jeering sexist pigs advancing towards women with mini-skirts. We rape. We abuse others, and each other. And the psycho-social context of this anti-social behaviour is scary: hangovers from a violent, police state; transmitting unhealthy social messages about what it means to be a man; living, frustrated, in a society that is grossly unequal. Where does one start to deal with such a mix of material, psychological and social causes underpinning sexual violence in our country? I am no shrink, or economist, and would not want to venture into the policy arena. But I feel it is important, based on my personal experiences, and observations, to encourage a discussion, as I have tried to do, but that we avoid. We must reflect on the questions that have preoccupied me here, 'Why are we like this? Why are we so violent?'

It was a commitment to talk about these realities that eventually led to me, about a year back, calling up my cousin to talk about him raping me. I was very nervous about the call. For years I had wondered whether I might not be misremembering my own childhood. So I could not rule out the possibility that my cousin would be shocked at what I had claimed he had done to me. Could I really be sure that my memory was reliable?

I decided, nevertheless, to call him.

'Hi. How are you?' My heart skipped a beat.

'Fine, UB, how are you? You're a big man now!' He chuckled. It was absolutely uncanny. He used to use the same playful, innocent chortle when he was a teenager and I was a little kid, to lure me – quite literally, I guess – into a false sense of trust. Now he was repeating the trick, no doubt instinctively, like all habitual sex offenders probably do. Old habits die hard.

'I'm fine thanks ... uhm, I really want to ask you something. I hope you don't mind. About what happened long ago?'

'Yes, you can ask UB. What is it?' He was speaking as gently as he used to when I had treated him like my older brother when he still lived with my family.

'Do you remember what you did to me?' I could not accuse him of wrongdoing directly. That still felt disingenuous, somehow. I could not think of myself as a victim even now. And yet I knew that I needed him to confirm that my mind was not playing tricks on me, that I was remembering the past reliably. That, more than confrontation, was the goal.

'Why are you bringing those things up now UB? Leave the past, cousin.' He responded very nonchalantly.

'But you remember, right?'

'Ja, we were children at that time, cousin.' He was a good seven or eight years older than me so it was a wee bit deceptive to pretend it was all child's play, nothing serious. But still I did not shout at him or confront him forthrightly. Instead, I got mild revenge with two blunt and hard-hitting questions I had wondered about for years.

'Are you attracted to little boys still? Have you ever done it to your son?' He was shocked at my directness. Actually, so was I. But I matched his nonchalance.

'No, those feelings were gone many years ago. I don't do those things anymore cousin. We were just kids. Cousin, I must wake up early tomorrow man. Let's chat again.'

And that was that. I remain clueless what the full range of responses to him should, perhaps, have been. Being a victim does not mean you're also an expert at healing. But what was clear to me, after putting the phone down, was that silence is not an option. I got something out of the conversation – confirmation, at the very least, that I did not have an overactive imagination. That alone is critical. Many women, and children, suffer in silence. So whatever professionals would say about how we should respond to violent sexualities, I am pretty sure that silence is unlikely to come out as a useful tool of engagement with our experiences. If we are to understand our fractured society, we need to talk.

We fear – I think – that understanding will lead to excusing, and so we reduce our chances of finding the right solutions because we tend to spend an inadequate amount of time reflecting on why we are who we are, and why we are what we have become. It is left to sterile academic journals to generate this conversation among experts when it is a conversation that also needs to happen, in fact, on our diary pages, in our families and within our communities.

It seems to me that whatever solutions experts might put on the table for how we might recover from our violent past, or how we might finally reduce inequality, one thing is certain: we cannot let boys and men off the moral hook.

Understanding does not mean excusing. I cannot excuse my older cousin's vicious, violent sexual assault on me even if he was not yet an adult (he was roughly fifteen years old or so at the time, and I was about seven). He was responsible enough, as a young model teenager, to be a student leader at his school, a top pupil, in charge of a youth group at his church. He knew the difference between right and wrong. He was not a machine that was programmed to do wrong. And so he is morally responsible for raping me.

Similarly, the boys and men who raped the Sowetan teenager cannot be excused because they are poor, or frustrated, or because they have experienced and observed violence in their homes, and have seen their dad and brothers role-modelling rapists. These social facts give us reason to show mercy, perhaps, when it comes to what punishment is meted out or what rehabilitation programmes offenders should be allowed to undergo. But these facts about violent boys' and men's lives do not give us reason to shout, '*not* guilty!'

To let me off the moral hook is to fail not just my victims but also to fail me, as a perpetrator, because letting me off the hook says, 'You could not help it! You're not fully human, you're just a robot! You're a victim, not a villain!'

We must expect morally decent behaviour from men and boys even in a time of deep inequality, poverty, joblessness – and in the shadow of a violent apartheid past. How we achieve a society in which boys and men are morally decent, of course, is a conversation we can no longer delay, unless we want to see more videos of women being gang-raped, or men recounting stories of being raped when they were young ...

SHOULD LOVERS HAVE SECRETS?

WHO SHOULD TAKE THE BLAME WHEN
PASSION TRUMPS RESPONSIBILITY?

WHEN SHOULD RELATIONSHIPS BE REGULATED?

THERE'S SOMETHING I HAVE TO TELL YOU

Falling in love is so bloody easy, isn't it? Mind you, falling in lust is way easier and we often confuse the two. But let's not be philosophical about things. The heart – bottom line – can sometimes overpower the head. That happened to me during a glorious 2005 summer while living in England. I met an American filmmaker at my favourite club, Bootylicious. I had watched him on the dance floor, and his energy was amazing. I felt like a lucky talent scout, and knew I had to sign up the talent, before someone else came along and beat me to it.

Maurice looked at me, and our eyes locked. The chemistry was instant, and, as gay life goes, we knew before even chatting to each other, that it would all end in an orgasmic explosion at mine, or his.

And that's exactly what went down. I woke up in a hotel room in central London, still as excited as I was when I had first seen him on the dance floor. He clearly felt the same. We chuckled at the recollection of just how much noise we had made in this tiny hotel. But, dammit, it was worth it. The sex was amazing! Turns out he was in London for the Gay and Lesbian Film Festival, and one of the main guests at the event, bringing with him his much talked-about feature film about black gay characters. He had to attend the festival that morning, and I had to go back to Oxford. But he invited me back to London for the final festival event as his 'plus one'. I couldn't wait. And thus our amazing transcontinental love affair started ...

The distance sucked. But we kept in touch by email, and Skype helped. We were like teenagers who had just discovered the naughtiness that adults get up to behind closed doors. He would write me darn good odes. I would respond with cheesy pseudo-poetry. I was greatly looking forward to seeing him again on a trip to New York that was due a few months later. It wasn't clear whether we were officially dating, but we knew this would be something we'd have to chat about, seriously, when we saw each other.

And so with a mixture of excitement and trepidation, I smiled as the plane touched down in New York. I was hoping for the best: Maurice was kind, intelligent, funny, energetic, compassionate and a bloody good lover. What more could I ask for? I was in New York on other business, but the plan was to stay a few days extra at his place in Brooklyn. And that's what I did.

After the first day, Maurice said we should go to some of the pubs in Soho. We had still avoided the talk about the status of our relationship. And so he suggested we go for a walk to the Hudson pier. We strolled carefully, holding hands, and I waited for him to speak. He was, after all, my host, and a little older than me! He turned around, and looked me in the eyes. I got scared, fearing he might propose marriage!

'There's something I have to tell you. I'm HIV-positive.'

I froze. Stunning silence. I had no clue what to say. After what felt like a lifetime, I found myself simply embracing him, giving him a long hug. And then, seconds later, the panic set in. We had penetrative sex in London without a condom. I was the receptive partner. I started shaking. I told him we should go home immediately. And that's what we did. We did not talk much on the train. I felt a mix of emotions ranging from fear, to sympathy for him, to utter numbness. But anger, it seemed, was not forthcoming. Until we got to the flat.

'Why didn't you tell me, Maurice?' I was now furious, especially because during one of our conversations he had asked me, funnily enough, but clearly deliberately, whether I would date someone who was HIV-positive. And I had said 'yes' without hesitation. I told him all the medical facts I knew, about friends of mine who are positive and healthy and just how irrational the stigma was. No-one could have had a better space in which to reveal their status.

'I was scared of rejection,' he mumbled.

'But, Maurice, even if that's true, why didn't you insist we use a condom? Insisting on a condom is not the same as revealing your status!' I shouted at him. He stormed out, only returning later. Meanwhile, I called one of my mentors in South Africa who is HIV-positive, and almost cried with fear.

He told me to remain calm, and asked the salient facts: what was Maurice's viral load? Was there an exchange of ejaculatory fluid? How rough was the sex? Was there any tearing of the tissue? Who was receptive? Was he on anti-retroviral drugs? We got the number for a clinic where I could get a test done. I got hold of Maurice, and we forged a temporary truce. Fortunately for me he was on treatment, had an undetectable viral load, and although the sex was rough, for some reason unrelated to his HIV status, he struggles to ejaculate, and distinctly remembered he did not ejaculate. So the odds were in my favour, from a purely medical and statistical viewpoint.

But the nervous system doesn't care for the odds.

I took the test the next day. Maurice went with me. We were told to call for the result in an hour. During that time Maurice and I sat quietly in Central Park. And then I called. My heart was pounding.

'What is your number, sir?' I gave the number.

'Your result is ... uhm ...' Just tell me, dammit! And then he did. And I simply collapsed on the ground, crying.

No-one forgets an experience like that. But I think of it when I read the mad public policy pseudo-debates around HIV. Some people, including politicians who ought to know better, think that the transmission of HIV should be criminalised. In other words, they think that if my test result was to have been positive, and Maurice knew he was positive but chose not to tell me, Maurice should be thrown in jail. I think that is a silly position, both in law but also from a public health point of view. Even though I was exposed to HIV by someone who did not tell me his status, I am still not convinced criminalisation makes sense. (And, for the record, I am not suffering from Stockholm syndrome! I fell out of love immediately, and resent him for not insisting on condom use.) But here is the reason for why I think that we should not criminalise the transmission of HIV.

First, our public health goal is clear. We want a decrease in the prevalence of HIV in our population. An important strategy for getting there is to slow down the rate at which HIV spreads. This requires us to encourage South Africans to get tested, and to know their status. It requires us to encourage South Africans not to fear living openly with HIV or AIDS. There is nothing worse for your immune system than anxiety. And if you fear stigma, losing your job, or being ostracised by your community, then you will suffer in silence, and that will simply hasten the onset of a weakened immune system.

If we criminalise the transmission of HIV, we simply feed the atmosphere of fear, and stigma. We make it less likely, not more likely, that citizens will voluntarily get tested and know their status. This is counter to the aim of public health policies on HIV/AIDS. It is particularly a bad idea given that enough research has shown that people who know their status actually – notwithstanding Maurice's behaviour – make more responsible sexual health decisions than those of us who do not test regularly or who do not know our current status. So it doesn't make public health sense, therefore, to implement a policy that would simply discourage people from getting tested.

Second, the most vulnerable group, black women, will suffer. Often those who punt the idea of throwing bastards into jail for spreading HIV think they are doing women a favour. But think about it. If there was a specific statutory law that targeted HIV-positive people, it would target mostly women, not men. Why? Because more black women, than men, know their status. This is because of the testing that happens as part of antenatal care. So the tragic irony is that such a law would actually worsen the lives of the most vulnerable group. Many spiteful male lovers could lay spurious charges against their female partners. There is proof of the woman's status. There is no proof that a man who never tested for HIV was positive all along. So it is useful to think about the impact of a law on the group you are trying to protect. Sometimes, as in this instance, good legislative intentions can go awry.

Third, such a law simply reinforces the myth that being HIV-positive means you are a dead man walking. It is not true. As well-known clinician Francois Venter said to me the other day, HIV is now a manageable chronic disease. It is more difficult to manage diabetes than HIV. And, if someone is on anti-retroviral drugs, and has an undetectable viral load, they are hardly infectious. By using statutory laws to deal with HIV transmission, you would simply be reinforcing medical myths about HIV.

Finally, as a piece of law, it would be a bad idea jurisprudentially. We have laws against murder because it is clear that if I pull the trigger and you die shortly thereafter my actions caused your death. The causal nexus is fairly obvious, and reasonably easy to prove. A statute about HIV would be very difficult to make sense of. Given that one can live a healthy life, for decades, if you take drugs, and take care of other aspects of your well-being, it is not clear what the wrongful act in law is that would be targeted by the statute. Beyond that, proving that someone had HIV and, in addition, that they knew they had HIV at the time of sexual intercourse, is an evidential burden that would be very difficult to meet, short of violating, for example, doctor-patient confidentiality. Given these legal hurdles, and the cost from a public health point of view, it is not worth even contemplating a specific statute to target HIV-positive people who have unprotected sex without revealing their status to a prospective sexual partner.

Does this mean I feel indifferent towards Maurice? No, it doesn't mean that. But it does mean that I am all too aware that there are wider social dynamics that must come into play here. For one thing, I am not a hapless victim. If I was raped, or if I was a woman being told that it is culturally compulsory to never say 'no' to a man wanting to penetrate me, then I might be a victim. But we cannot assume that all of us who get exposed to possible infection with HIV are victims. I voluntarily had sex with Maurice without a condom. And while he had an ethical duty to disclose his status, I also had an obligation towards myself to make responsible sexual health decisions.

We seem to struggle to know how to balance the different

responsibilities of sexual partners. There is no doubt in my mind that, at the very least, Maurice had a moral duty to insist on using a condom so that he did not expose me to undue harm. But what is woefully absent from the public and popular clamour at times to criminalise the transmission of HIV, is a full and fair discussion of the distribution of duties between sexual partners. Ultimately, I have to take responsibility for having unprotected sex.

Furthermore, we need to reflect on the limits of the law. We are in danger of becoming as law obsessed as the Americans. Sure, legal instruments are crucial, especially in a country where there is plenty wrong with the fabric of society. But just as laws that protect gay people cannot effectively eliminate homophobic attitudes towards gay men and women, so, too, laws criminalising HIV will not deal with the stigma surrounding HIV/AIDS. That requires moral and political leadership, civil society initiatives within the community, and conversations among citizens, and in our homes. That is how, slowly, we will educate boys and men that women are not their property. And that is how we will help women to break free from cultural shackles that put undue pressure on them. These are social challenges, and the law is a blunt instrument with which to try to address them.

Love, and making love, in a time of HIV is not easy. But medical facts, and not myth, should inform how we respond to this public health challenge. Mass hysteria is pointless.

?

DO WOMEN IN POLYGAMOUS MARRIAGES
NEED RESCUING?

WHY DO YOU INSTINCTIVELY OPPOSE POLYGAMY?

IS POLYGAMY REALLY WORSE THAN MANY MARRIAGES?

IF YOU'RE A LIBERAL, WHY DON'T YOU LIKE POLYGAMY?

I love the ongoing debate about polygamy. It is one of the issues that underscores the deep ideological divisions in our nation. (I write about these divisions more generally in 'A divided nation'.) And let me be clear upfront: I think polygamy is morally acceptable, quite apart from the fact that it is legally permissible.

I am always amused by people's reaction to my position. And by that I do not mean their reaction to my reasons for holding the position. I mean their reactions simply to the fact that I hold the viewpoint at all.

Some people think I take the piss; that I must be insincere when I say I think polygamy is morally okay. Others think I am simply behaving like the trained, competitive debater that I am; that I am trying to show off an ability to defend any position. Still others think it is not surprising I have this view; after all, what else could you expect from a gay man? And then there are many of my liberal friends who are horrified; they think that I simply misunderstand liberal freedom if I imagine that 'anything goes' in a liberal society. For these friends I am an amusing but mildly embarrassing poster child for liberalism when I loudly make the case for polygamy.

Yet, my viewpoint is one I hold with utter sincerity. Reactions to my viewpoint, for me, just are an indication of how hardened we all are when it comes to moral and cultural beliefs and intuition. We are so convinced of the obviousness of our own positions that someone we 'respect' or are friends with who holds a contrary view must be insincere, taking the piss, being contrarian, or misunderstanding their own worldview. Not so. That is why I want to explain, with a necessary dash of – cough – sincerity, why I think polygamy is morally acceptable.

THE LIBERAL CASE

Most defenders of polygamy usually appeal to tradition. They think that since polygamy has existed for a long time, and has structured the lives of many in parts of our country, it is morally acceptable.

I don't like this argument. Appeals to culture, or any habit, are weak. One needs to say why a culture is valuable independent of the fact that it is has been around for a long time. Misogyny has been around for a long time, and yet that does not make it morally acceptable. Homophobia remains popular, and has been popular forever, and yet it is morally unacceptable to be homophobic. So I do not – like many who hold my view – think that the correct basis for accepting polygamy is that it is a tradition with old roots.

I think polygamy is morally acceptable because it is my duty as a liberal to accept polygamy. My viewpoint stems from my general commitment to liberalism. A liberal society is one that values the autonomy of individuals. This means that each individual is allowed to make choices that are in accordance with their most deeply-held values and beliefs. The role of the state, and fellow citizens, is to interfere with your freedom as little as possible so that you can express your autonomy in your choices of careers, studies, where you live, and so forth. That is the kind of society we have chosen for ourselves and, also, as a glorious break from the illiberal apartheid state we used to live under.

'Freedom' and 'autonomy' are values that we must respect at all times. We should only ever restrict freedom when someone tries to use their freedom to rob someone else of their freedom. That is why we don't allow murder, for example. I cannot use my freedom to take someone else's freedom away by killing them.

In summary: as a liberal society we rightly err on the side of allowing maximum freedom for all and restrict freedom only in very limited cases. And in those limited cases where we restrict freedom we do so precisely because we value freedom.

It follows quite straightforwardly, surely, that if five adults choose to enter into a polygamous relationship, then that is morally acceptable. Doing so is simply an expression of their autonomy.

Just because most of us are raised to think that the ideal relationship model is that of one man and one woman does not mean that model is in fact the only morally acceptable one. So long as consenting adults are not coerced, why should they not be allowed to be part of a polygamous relationship? I see no reason why a liberal society should stop adults from entering into a polygamous relationship.

In fact, this is not just about liberalism. Since there is no harm to bystanders, there is little reason why any society should disapprove of polygamous relationships.

BUT ... BUT!

The only acceptable 'objection' to polygamy is actually not a real objection. People often say to me, 'But ... but ... only men are allowed to do it! Women are not allowed to have more than one husband!' That is true. But that is not an argument against polygamy. It is simply a reason to change our customary laws so that they are less inconsistent in their treatment of different relationships. There is no reason why women should not be allowed to marry more than one man. And there is no reason why men should not be allowed to marry more than one man. And, yes, there is no reason why women should not be allowed to marry more than one woman. Polyandry, and polyamorous relationships more generally, should be recognised by the law.

When gay men and women fought to be allowed to get married, the demand certainly was not that marriage laws should be scrapped. The fight was rather to correct our laws so that these laws stopped discriminating against gay couples unfairly. Similarly, the fact that only men can marry more than one female partner in customary law is no reason to throw the polygamous baby out with the dirty legal water. The solution is to have the law recognise all of these different kinds of relationships. Of course this is unlikely to happen. But the fact that it is unlikely to happen tells us just how deeply entrenched current social convictions are.

There is no way a law will be passed in my lifetime allowing me to marry more than one man. But that doesn't mean polygamy is immoral. That simply means the law is immoral. It is immoral because it treats heterosexual men, in relationships recognised by civil law, as more special than the rest of us. We must, however, always be careful that we don't use legal discrepancies as an unfair basis for rejecting a particular practice.

WOMEN ARE NOT FREE

The most serious, and most genuine, concern about polygamy I've come across is the fear that most women in these relationships are not genuinely free. There is, so the argument goes, no meaningful sense in which they freely enter these relationships. They are often under family or community pressure, and experience a kind of cultural duress. Women in these relationships, even when they smile broadly, are actually, secretly, very unfree. If we put it differently, we might say that if they have real options they would surely not have chosen to enter into an arrangement in which they are simply the property of men who use them as a means to an end.

Just as sex workers would surely rather make money through other means, so a woman in a polygamous relationship would, ideally, not be in a polygamous relationship. Like the sex worker, women in polygamous relationships aren't really free.

I find this concern both unconvincing and (though well-meaning) deeply condescending. The first and perhaps the most interesting problem with it is that it assumes that women have a better deal under the current relationship schemes that we promote socially and allow legally. But this is empirically, to the best of my knowledge, not established. And anecdotally it is certainly flimsy. Women in 'ordinary' marriages between one man and one woman also often come out pretty badly too, literally and figuratively. The institution of marriage is just not good for women's genuine – whatever that means – liberation. It is an institution that was historically designed to ensure women were something of a means to men's ends. And of course many women are not trapped in marriages these days. We have to acknowledge feminist gains, and social mores having evolved to some extent.

But here's the point: those who oppose polygamy simply assume that women in monogamous relationships are necessarily happier than women in polygamous relationships. Yet, when divorce (flowing from monogamous marriages) happens it is mostly women and not men that are left financially crippled, still. And it is still more often than not the woman who stays at home or who has to double-up as both career wife and parent shouldering disproportionate domestic chores. And many women have to put up with philandering husbands, and domestic abuse, both physical and emotional. Monogamous relationships, and monogamous marriages, are not exactly kind to many women.

No-one ever bothers asking women in polygamous relationships how they feel or how they evaluate their lives. The fervent assumption is that anyone is obviously better off in a monogamous relationship.

I would have thought that if we were thinking consistently and clearly we should, in the worst-case scenario, conclude that both monogamous and polygamous relationships are generally bad for women. In which case we should either reject all relationships between men and women, or, if we put up with monogamy despite the poor treatment of many women in monogamous relationships, then we also have to accept polygamy. Unless, of course, consistency is not something we value, in which case I can be ignored.

I claimed that there is an aspect of this objection to polygamy that I find condescending. It is this. The idea that no woman could – or would – ever choose to enter polygamous relationships 'freely' seems to be an assumption that treats any woman in such a relationship as a victim, as a child. It is the same condescension that often creeps into debate about sex work – that no woman is truly free if she chooses sex work. The worry is not just that women are poorly treated in polygamous relationships. It is a stronger claim – that we can say, without even speaking to her, that a woman in such a relationship is not thinking clearly or is a victim of her community. But this surely cannot be correct. It seems that the social disapproval of polygamy, especially from middle class South Africans, is so strong that it leads opponents of the practice to inadvertently have a condescending attitude towards the very people – women – they are trying to help. In rather twisted irony, opponents of polygamy end up showing as little regard for women as many men who genuinely regard women as incapable of having a valid opinion of their own about themselves.

The analogy with sex work is useful. It doesn't matter how sassy, how confident, how in charge of her life a particular sex worker looks and sounds, some opponents of sex work just cannot get themselves to believe that sex workers are 'truly' free. It is clear to me that this refusal is not a reflection of the fact that sex work is genuinely a form of social imprisonment under conditions of job scarcity. There is simply a stubborn refusal to acknowledge that many women have not lost their agency, but really do choose, under conditions of job scarcity or not, to be sex workers. This refusal is more a reflection of irrational and persistent middle class prejudice by and large, and less a reflection of justified empathy for women living necessarily horrid lives. Polygamy, similarly, results in excessive and unjust 'empathy' for women who are not living lives fundamentally different, in terms of levels of psycho-social well-being, from those of us who are single, or in monogamous relationships. How often, though, do we pity the woman whose monogamous marriage ends in ruins because her husband is a cheat? Yet we pity the women in polygamous relationships even when many of them do not exhibit the unhappiness of the lonely soccer mum in the suburbs.

I am certainly not suggesting that all women in polygamous relationships are happy. I cannot say that in the absence of robust empirical evidence. My point is simpler, but crucial still as a response to opponents of polygamy. Bad relationships are bad for women. Bad relationships can be monogamous or they can be polygamous. That is the real point, and the reason we should stop singling out polygamy as uniquely or particularly bad for women.

OBJECTS OF MEN'S SATISFACTION?

What about the concern that women in polygamous relationships are simply used as a means to an end by men? Men use them and treat them as objects, often for their sexual satisfaction, as indications of wealth and status, and as extra hands for domestic chores. This is the core of the inherent immorality of these relationships, someone might say.

I think one problem with this argument is that it is a variation on what has already been discussed, a bald assertion that any pressures women face – sexually, psychologically or otherwise – in polygamous relationships are worse than the levels of pressure in monogamous relationships. I see no reason why this is necessarily true.

There is, in addition, a more subtle difficulty here. It is a difficulty that in some way goes beyond the polygamy debate. Somewhere along the line we convinced ourselves that being used as a means to an end is always a bad thing. It is not. But I had better explain myself. If men never wanted to use me as a means to an end I would be depressed. If someone is attracted to me sexually, part of what that means is that they want to jump me, and, like an animal, they want to make love to me until they climax sexually and then get off me again. The desire to use someone else to help you come to a sexual climax is natural. Equally, wanting to evoke that kind of feeling in someone else is also natural. This is why, in part, many of us worry about our bodies, how we dress, how we sound, etc. We want others not only to desire to use us as a means to an end; we want them to actually do so. I would probably end up paying a shrink a lot of money to come to terms with a life in which no-one uses me as a means to an end!

So we should get over the slogan, 'Don't use other people as a means to an end!' What we really mean is something else. We should always respect each other. But you can respect someone and still want to jump them. And in that sense there is no logical opposition between respecting someone and having a sexual desire to use them as a means to an end. Whether you respect someone or not can't be determined by answering the question, 'Do you want to use them sexually?' (Obviously one might argue that some men are utterly self-absorbed, and so perhaps not respectful. But I want to leave that aside. The point is that in our ordinary thinking and way of speaking about sex we have lazily assumed, for the most part, that wanting to use someone for sexual purposes is wrong. And I think this is lazy because once we think about this kind of claim seriously enough we realise we don't really mean it! Unless we are asexual, of course ...)

So, if a man in a polygamous relationship wants to use his wives as a means to sexual satisfaction, that is fine. In fact, if I was a woman in such a relationship, I would be more concerned if he never wanted me to be part of his sexual life. That would be worse for my self-esteem. I just don't see, therefore, the pulling power of the concern that men in polygamous relationships have a secret desire to be sexually satisfied by their wives. The only objection would be if the women were forced to have sex with him, but it goes without saying that this would be wrong, and, more importantly, it would be an objection to any form of forced sexual engagement regardless of the kind of relationship framing it. It is, again, not polygamy that is the enemy here. It is coercion. And I just don't see why opposition to coerced sexual activity should be confused with polygamy.

It is clear, I hope, that most opponents of polygamy are inconsistent in how they think about the fate of women. They often turn a blind eye to the suffering of women in monogamous relationships but have a lot to say about the supposed intrinsic moral wrongs of polygamous relationships. This inconsistency, in my view, is not innocent. It reflects a few things: a) that we are socialised to regard monogamous relationships as an acceptable norm even when these relationships are empirically no less rewarding for women than other relationships; and b) that opposition to polygamy is not really principled but ultimately aesthetic: polygamy seems backward, illiberal, and from a time and a place that should have no resonance in a new, liberal, post-democratic society.

The greatest irony, however, is that anyone who is interested in thinking about liberalism carefully would actually come to a different conclusion. It is this: liberalism demands that we all accept polygamy. If anything, we should go a step further and also endorse polyandry. But, sadly, we don't live in a society in which clear moral thought is routine, let alone reflected in our laws. That's not polygamy's fault. That's the fault of poor public discourse, and a gap between law and morality. Polygamy should be left alone.

ulture

WHY ARE SOUTH AFRICANS SO DESPERATE TO CLING TO THE IDEA OF A RAINBOW NATION?

WHY ARE WE AFRAID OF DEEP DIFFERENCES?

ISN'T NATIONALISM OVERRATED?

A DIVIDED NATION

I sometimes feel very sorry for us. We have an almost pathological yearning as South Africans to be Archbishop Desmond Tutu's (in)famous rainbow nation, the image that propelled us into the new South Africa. Since then, it has by and large been left up to big sporting events to sustain the rainbow nation lie – the Rugby World Cup of 1995 is still the most nostalgia inducing of the lot, followed a close second by our successful hosting of the 2010 Soccer World Cup. There's nothing like sporting madness to make us feel united. You'd have to be a real party-pooper not to get a knot in your throat at the sight of white Afrikaans Blue Bulls supporters on beer crates in Soweto.

Well, optical illusions will get us nowhere. True unity – whatever it amounts to – must be grounded, firmly, in reality. So allow me to burst the bubble: South Africa is a divided nation.

We are spatially, linguistically, culturally and ideologically divided. And it is best we come to grips with this reality sooner rather than later.

THE SPATIAL DIVIDES

It fascinates me that so many of us resist my viewpoint that we are divided when we can't even live together. In the title essay of this collection ('A Bantu in my bathroom!'), I told the story of an elderly white lady who could not imagine living in the same house as a black person. That was one example of a much bigger spatial apartheid story we are still in the grips of. My hometown, Grahamstown, is a perfect example. It is such a small city and yet you could easily live your entire life there having very little contact with people different from yourself. The only multiracial, multiclass near-contact point is the city centre where everyone does their shopping. Beyond that very small part of the city, there is a huge spatial divide between the different communities of the City of Saints.

My high school, Graeme College Boys' High, for example, is situated in what was an affluent white suburb. (It is still affluent, but less white now.) I landed up in this school only because the nun running my primary school had insisted my parents 'sacrifice' every penny to make sure my academic potential was not wasted on the weak, local coloured high school. Travelling to school every day felt like being bused from one country to another, from the poor, Afrikaans-speaking coloured township to the wealthy, English-speaking white suburb. The city was planned in accordance with the demands of the Group Areas Act of 1950. Blacks, coloureds, whites and Indians were geographically separated. This is still the case for the most part.

In standard seven, our geography teacher, Mr Freeman, walked us to a little koppie just above the school where we could see the town's contours very clearly. A dry little stream in the horizon separated the coloured township from the black township. That was the buffer that was mandated by the apartheid city planners. Grahamstown residents don't live in each other's spaces. They live *around* each other. And the rest of the country is no different. We are geographically, spatially, divided as a nation.

My family still lives in the coloured neighbourhood. My two sisters have teenage children, Rolando and Regine. Rolando and Regine have only coloured friends. They attend the local school in the community, Mary Waters High School, which is overwhelmingly attended by only coloured children. Rolando and Regine, although teenagers, have never had proper social contact with children of other race, language or class backgrounds. And the children and families in the neighbourhood where they are growing up, look and sound like them, listen to the same music as them, enjoy the same kinds of cuisine, watch the same soap operas, and date and marry each other.

They live in a homogenous poor, coloured, Afrikaans, conservative, Christian bubble.

My siblings and nephews and nieces are not the exception to some grand, national integration success story. They are living the lives of the majority of South Africans. We live apart from each other. There is a very small number of South Africans who defy these spatial patterns, and even these 'exceptions' are misunderstood.

Often, for example, townhouse complexes in the northern suburbs of Johannesburg are glorified as exemplars of what can happen when people see beyond race and learn to live in each other's space.

But of course this is disingenuous. You can live in the same neighbourhood as people who look and sound different from yourself and still be divided. Just the other day, for example, I was taking a stroll around my fenced-in complex. A white lady stepped outside of her flat and walked in my direction. She spotted me and looked like she knew she had just met her rapist or murderer. The fear was palpable. She scurried back inside like a nervous rat. I was furious, deeply furious at the assumption that a burly black man must be dangerous until proven otherwise. A few minutes later she emerged behind her security gate and nervously asked, 'Do you live here?'

'No, I am from the moon, and you?' I snapped back and walked off. That kind of experience is not unfamiliar and shatters the myth that pockets of integration are happening and are leading to social cohesion in 'the suburbs'.

I have been guilty of similarly anti-social behaviour. At the first complex where I had lived, I stayed next to an Indian couple for more than a year. The entrance to their front door was less than a ruler's distance from mine. We always smiled at each other. Sometimes I saw them at the gym, and the smile festival continued. Sometimes the wonderful aroma of curries would flow in through my front door and I knew that if this was in the township I would have been able to walk next door and get my plate! But I was left 'respecting their space' since that seemed to be the unspoken mores around there. One day I heard a baby crying – I realised the couple had had their first baby. Every single member of the extended families arrived over the weekend. Did I dare to congratulate them on their bundle of joy? No. And I am supposed to be a first generation coconut, the product of multicultural schooling.

These are the hard facts about us. We live in different neighbourhoods, and those of us who live in the same neighbourhood often fake integration to mask deeper divisions in our lived realities, and in our personal identities. You get along with the guy at the office whose name has a click in it, so you cannot possibly be said to be uncomfortable with people of another racial, cultural or linguistic background, right? Such is the complexity of our self-deception.

But spatial apartheid, and nifty avoidance techniques, tell a different story. I still don't know the names of the Indian couple who smiled at me for a year.

THE LINGUISTIC – AND CULTURAL – DIVIDES

In addition to our spatial divisions we are also linguistically divided. I speak English and Afrikaans fluently. Despite being from the Eastern Cape, and having a Xhosa stepmother, I did not bother learning Xhosa. Being the good liberal that I am, I did take a non-mother tongue Xhosa course during my undergraduate years at Rhodes University, but I am simply not fluent. My little brother, who has a Xhosa heritage, is fully trilingual. He speaks English, Afrikaans and Xhosa very well, and code switches within these languages more fluently than I can. For example, he speaks a very different kind of English – more grammatically correct stuff – with me than he does with his coloured friends who tend to translate very directly from Afrikaans – 'Daddy did take me to the beach!' rather than 'Daddy took me to the beach!' The fact that he speaks 'properly' when he chats with me is an indication of the fact that he consciously switches between dialects. He chooses to use certain slang words, and certain localised rules of speech, when speaking to his friends that don't apply to our communication.

This is also an example of how language is about more than mere communication. Language is also about identity. My little brother loves rap, especially the music of coloured rappers from coloured townships in Port Elizabeth and the Cape Flats. These rappers rap in English but in the kind of dialect and slang that he uses when he communicates with his friends. And they rap about their own lived realities, which are different from mine, and with which I cannot really identity, even though I am coloured too.

There are a few important lessons here. Languages both facilitate communication and constitute part of our identities. But the consequence of this fact is that if we do not speak each other's languages then we are not bridging cultural divides between ourselves. This is quite apart from not being able to communicate effectively with each other.

A large number of South Africans are admirably multilingual. But they tend to be mostly black Africans. Most white, Indian and coloured South Africans are either monolingual or bilingual, mostly speaking English and Afrikaans. One consequence of this is that the linguistic divides in the country inadvertently also reinforce racial, class and cultural divides. If I cannot speak Xhosa, it is more difficult for me to successfully challenge explicit and latent prejudices I might have towards Xhosa people.

While many black Africans are fluent in English and Afrikaans too, that simply reinforces the fact that one can be – as political analyst Aubrey Matshiqi often puts it – in the numerical majority but still be in the cultural minority. Put simply, black Africans come to the language party more often than their white, Indian and coloured counterparts. That, too, reinforces rather than narrows distances between us because it is a reminder of the social hierarchy of languages in our society: English and Afrikaans, stemming from our racist past, were always deemed more important than indigenous African languages.

To point out, as many often do at this point, that English is necessary as a common medium of communication, and the international language of commerce, is to miss the point. If your gardener with fewer educational opportunities than you can speak fluently to you in English, and go back home and speak five languages, why are you too arrogant to challenge yourself for being monolingual?

The linguistic divide, for the reason I just explained, inevitably coincides with racial divisions in our country. That's to be expected. But it is also not quite that neat. The linguistic divisions between my little brother and me are real, and yet it is not a black and white affair. If I don't bother making sense of his dialect of English and Afrikaans, then I rob myself of an opportunity of getting to know him better, to get inside his headspace.

I actually got him to download some of his favourite rap onto my iPod and there is little doubt that dancing to his tunes helped to close the linguistic – and therefore cultural – divide between us as brothers. In the absence of that kind of effort, linguistic divisions are powerful obstacles to learning to live with each other and not just around each other. For the most part, however, we do not, as a country, make sufficient effort to close the linguistic divisions that exist in the country. Shockingly, for example, it remains a (controversial) education policy pipedream whether or not it should be compulsory for learners to be taught at least one African language in schools. This should be a no-brainer. But it isn't, precisely because the nature and consequences of the linguistic divide are so poorly understood by many of us.

THE IDEOLOGICAL DIVIDES

One of the clearest examples of our ideological division as South Africans are different attitudes towards our constitution. I absolutely love our constitution. I think it is an incredibly progressive document that takes freedom seriously. It is a vision of the kind of society we are trying to build in our post-democracy, a society in which the rights of individuals and communities are respected and protected from a tyranny of the majority.

From a philosophical perspective, however, the constitution is a profoundly liberal document, one that at its core is based on liberal individualism. Of course it is true that there are clauses that refer to communities and society at large, but in the evolving jurisprudence that has come out of the Constitutional Court since 1996, it has mostly been the freedom of individuals and minorities – including, to be precise, the *individual* members of majority groups – that has come out tops in key cases, especially ones centred on social policy or lifestyle issues. It is in part with the help of the normative vision of this profoundly liberal document that I have, in recent times, fiercely defended artist Brett Murray's right to offend President Jacob Zuma. (I air the specific issues around that event more fully in 'The People versus Brett Murray'.)

But liberals live in a bubble. In that bubble we celebrate the constitution but we refuse to deal with the reality that it is a profoundly contested document, a contestation that doesn't get much airplay only because the conservatives do not have access to public platforms, including the mainstream media, and many simply do not have the ability to make a case for their own ideological sidelining. And so, for example, I had to face a question in the middle of a symposium about artistic freedom from an audience member listening to my soliloquy about liberalism, 'Eusebius, do you think the constitution reflects the views of the majority?'

I think he was hoping to expose me for being hopelessly in love with our jurisprudence. He knew the answer to his own question. So I called his bluff, since I have always been comfortable with the realities about our constitutional dispensation. 'No. And you know the answer to that question anyway. The constitution is a profoundly liberal document. And most South Africans are deeply conservative. If we had referenda, most South Africans would probably allow the spanking of kids in our schools, do away with gay marriage, bring back the death penalty, and perhaps even reconsider abortion rights!'

We are scared of acknowledging this ideological divide. I suppose one reason for not talking about it is the fear that there is no way of settling moral and ideological differences, so why chat about it at all? It is better to simply hope that it will all disappear. The other reason is that liberals fear they might lose the debate, at least numerically, but they – we – are so convinced by the correctness of our worldview that we would rather find ways of 'educating' the majority of South Africans, to rid them of their ideological waywardness, than to risk our precious liberal constitutional edifice being challenged or, worse, reviewed and changed.

None of this conflict avoidance, however, changes the reality: we are an ideologically divided bunch.

SO WHAT SHOULD WE DO WITH OUR DIVISIONS?

If we are spatially, linguistically and ideologically divided – quite apart from our political divisions which are less in need of exposition – then it raises the question of why we are so desperate, as I discussed at the outset, to cling on to the idea of a united nation in which we all get along?

One reason we cling to motifs of 'oneness' is because we are scared that deep disagreement will perpetuate historical divisions. This, sadly, does not help to build a robust new society. It simply leads to fake unity that threatens to collapse when pressure is brought to bear on it, such as during the weeks of debate around 'The Spear' painting. We should, in fact, strive to build a democracy in which deep disagreement is possible.

I was struck by this fear of disagreement recently. At a public seminar hosted by Wits University, I accused liberals of not always standing up for what they believe in (especially in the face of black anger). An older, white member of the audience took issue with me during the discussion session. 'I want to challenge what Eusebius said about liberals. First, the only black person I am scared of is my wife!' (You have to love the liberal – nonchalantly prefacing such a question with the insistence that he must be progressive on account of an interracial marriage. Give the man a Bell's for effort!)

'I am also, might I add, friends with Advocate Malindi and felt for him when he broke down.' Advocate Malindi, of course, is the advocate who burst into tears during the urgent interdict application in court seeking to bar the Brett Murray painting of Zuma from being further exhibited.

'We have to understand the raw racial wounds we are still nursing!' the gentleman pleaded. He got some applause for sincerity, and no doubt sincere *agreement* from many in the audience.

But, as I pointed out to him, I am not callous enough to say we should not try to walk a mile in each other's shoes. Of course we should, and we will better live together in this fractured country of ours if we did that.

'The true test of our democratic maturation is not whether we can have many more "Kumbaya" moments but whether we can disagree deeply!'

Why should I pretend, for example, that I don't have deep ideological disagreements with conservative South Africans? We can laugh over a beer without talking about these, but the inevitable public policy moments will come along later and expose this pseudo-agreement. The goal, difficult to achieve in practice, must be to disagree deeply and still be able to share a beer (or a beer crate in Soweto).

The sooner we abandon the myth of a rainbow nation, a united nation, the better for our democracy. A national identity is neither necessary nor possible: we live in a diverse country with individuals and communities that have profoundly different beliefs, attitudes, habits and ideological convictions. Why insist on a common national identity? The fruitless search for a common national identity is not admirable. It is merely a symptom of a child so bruised and battered by her past that she wants to live in a future that is filled only with jingles. That is understandable, but the wrong goal. We should instead accept that we are deeply divided – spatially, linguistically, culturally, ideologically – and reflect on how we might live in each other's space while disagreeing deeply with each other. The alternative, fake national unity, is simply childish.

WHY IS THE PENIS SO SCARY?

_____

DO WE REALLY HAVE TO RESPECT A TITLE?

_____

DO SOUTH AFRICANS REALLY UNDERSTAND ART?

_____

THE PEOPLE VERSUS BRETT MURRAY

It is mindboggling just how prudish we are. It is also embarrassing how little art education there is in our society. The extreme vilification that artist Brett Murray has had to endure from political bullies and ordinary South Africans alike proves this. All because he dared to create a portrait of President Jacob Zuma complete with penis showing, and had it displayed in the Goodman Gallery in Rosebank in Johannesburg as part of a larger exhibition with political themes.

The criticisms have been both voluminous, and ferociously thoughtless. The work has been labelled racist and sadistic – courtesy of the South African Communist Party (SACP) – and an assault on the president's dignity, not to mention an assault on the office of the presidency. One political party's youth league leader, Buti Manamela from the SACP, insisted he would organise a march on the gallery to rip out the artwork, and even the minister of justice, Jeff Radebe, weighed in, suggesting that a criminal charge of *crimen injuria* be laid against the artist and possibly the gallery's management. (It was tempting to join Manamela's march with a placard shouting, FREE WILLY!)

These political bullies got a surprising amount of support from many ordinary South Africans, with social media sites being the preferred platform to express their disgust. Typical themes included persistent remarks that the work was in poor taste. Even Zuma's worst critics agreed, like *Business Day* editor, Peter Bruce, who reflected in his weekly column on just how shockingly unacceptable the artwork was, remarking, 'I cannot for the life of me understand what [Zuma] has done to deserve to be immortalised in a painting with his genitals hanging out of his trouser.' Strong stuff from someone who is a self-confessed member of the 'ABZ camp' – the Anything-But-Zuma camp. Many agreed with Bruce, arguing that the portrait did not help us with our nation-building project; it was divisive and disrespected the morality of the majority.

As a writer, and as a liberal South African who obsesses about the constitutional democracy that we have chosen as a break from an unfree past, my heart is shattered by this assault on artistic freedom. Raw political emotion and slander have been aggressively poured out as substitute for a sensible reflection on aesthetics.

IN DEFENCE OF THE CHEEKY ARTIST

My first real encounter with an art form was when I was nine. I signed up for piano and recorder lessons. For the next ten years I was a dedicated classical music student. I practised for hours every day, and with the nurturing of some brilliant music teachers – Mrs Higgins, Ms McNamee, Ms Spriggs (who became Mrs Grant), Mrs Hacksley and Mr Holder – I developed a deep love and respect for the role of the artist in society.

On a very personal level, playing the piano was escapist. I could lose myself in the frustration of learning ever more complicated scales and arpeggios, and technically difficult pieces with each year's progress. But it wasn't just the competitive me that found joy in these challenges. As a child, who grew up in a poor and violent family and neighbourhood, I could emote at the piano. It was little wonder, with so much stored emotion that never got released in the family home, that I was particularly obsessed with romantic and impressionist works. My two favourite composers, unsurprisingly, were Debussy and Chopin. And much to the annoyance of my piano teachers, I insisted on playing even Bach and Mozart pieces with the emotional depth of an impressionist work, even when these Baroque guys had written mostly for the dull harpsichord with its restrictions on interpretive range. Nothing would deter vulnerable little Eusebius McKaiser from feeling every musical piece. I could not show emotion at home without inviting a fat *klap*. So I had better get it all out at school during piano practice.

My self-indulgent relationship with the piano became more mature, and less me-focused, towards the end of high school. That was as a result of Mr Holder's 'History of Music' lessons that formed part of my matric music curriculum. I suddenly had to read about the lives and times of the musicians, so as to understand the social contexts in which their works were created. In addition, and as part of that intellectual engagement with the life of the composers, I also had to learn to negotiate the parallels between classical music and other genres of art, such as literature, painting and sculpting. Artists often engage each other inter-textually, and as a broader community, and so my narrow world of simply sitting down to play suddenly became much bigger. In fact, my love of history suddenly collided with my love of classical music.

The penny really dropped when Mr Holder regaled me with stories of the relationship between Russian composers and the Soviet regime. Composers like Dmitri Shostakovich were often accused of not showing sufficient political zeal and had to prove their patriotism – lest they were denied government support or had their works vilified. And so many majestic Russian symphonies that fill us, as casual listeners, with fire and joy, are actually products of a Russian political agenda rather than honest works of art that reflect the true feelings and creative direction of their creators. Melancholy was not allowed; majestic, nationalistic fervour was politically demanded. Our own neighbour, Zimbabwe, exhibits this callous relationship between the dictatorial state and state broadcasters in particular. Artists are manipulated: they are forced to help prop up the lie that all is well in Zimbabwe. They are trapped. They are not allowed to be the conscience of the nation.

These childhood lessons have stuck with me for life. They have had a lifelong impact on me. I have a special space in my heart for the artist. The artist – whether a classical music composer, a cartoonist like our own Zapiro, or a subversive painter like Brett Murray – must be allowed to produce artistic works that selfishly, but sincerely, represent the world as they see and experience it. Sincerity is the lifeblood of artworks of integrity.

Artists reflect back to us the world in which we live. They challenge us, engage our received beliefs and handed-down wisdoms. They have a thankless task, really – to keep us honest while all the while knowing they may have rotten apples thrown at them for upsetting the consensus.

This doesn't mean that an artist must be contrarian just for the sake of stirring. The only normative requirement that any artist should religiously stick to, in my view, is to produce works that are sincere.

Sometimes this will lead to a socially challenging work, like JM Coetzee's *Disgrace*. On other occasions, it will naturally produce stuff of nationalistic feel-good variety, like Mango Grooves' patriotic tracks that got us through the dying moments of apartheid – music filled with the promise of tomorrow's freedom and joy. But whether the product is jarring or reassuring is irrelevant: the artist must just be allowed to be.

And this is why the abuse hurled at Brett Murray is misplaced. It stems from bizarre, nationalist assumptions about the role of the artist in society. There is no duty on artists to produce works that will be good for national unity. That kind of jingoism is more fitting in Soviet Russia, and in a collapsing Zimbabwe. It is not appropriate in a South Africa that takes seriously the content and point of artistic freedom.

It is difficult not to be reminded of some politicians' profound irritation with *Disgrace*. The novel graphically captures tensions in the Eastern Cape, in the farming community especially, around the time of South Africa's transition towards democracy. It deals uncomfortably with themes like white guilt – even employing rape as a metaphor for exploring retribution – and nakedly presents interracial fears. Concerns about the work's place in schools were suddenly raised. The worry was that the black characters in the novel were not inspirational. They appeared flat or, at best, like savages ready to exact revenge.

Although the author is a recluse, one of his reported reasons for leaving South Africa and settling for Australia was, in part, disappointment at how the democratic government responded to his freedom of expression, by attempting to bully him into patriotic submission. We cannot prescribe to writers how to see the world. If we did that, we may as well reduce them to glorified typists while we dictate to them the words and thoughts of their literary characters.

If political leaders, or ordinary folk in society, want to work towards a nationalist project of building bridges, they must do so independently of telling artists what they must do. If a particular artist happens, by pure coincidence, to share a rainbow nation goal, then of course he or she could then produce the kinds of work that happen to also promote certain nationalist goals. But the key guiding principle here remains sincerity. If an artist is not sincere, they lack artistic integrity. (The only exception is when you produce works that are commissioned by someone or an institution willing to pay – but we hardly take these commercial creations as revealing the intellectual heart of an artist.) Jingoistic demands should be resisted.

Different genres of art have particular roles in society. Political cartoonists, unsurprisingly, ridicule and lampoon political events, decisions and political actors. They are social commentators just like social and political analysts who use words, rather than drawings, to comment on society. But, unlike analysts, they also use humour, sarcasm, wit and other critical devices to make their point. They have a similar space for using these devices as do stand-up comedians. We all know they play this role, and should therefore engage with their works on the basis that they represent one more form of social and political dialogue.

Yet, tragicomically, those people hurling abuse at Brett Murray simply expose their own lack of basic artistic education. One can only hope that newspapers do not report on the jokes of some of our top national stand-up comedians like Loyiso Gola and Trevor Noah. Many of the political jokes in our comedy clubs are, actually, much crasser, and harsher, than a portrait of Jacob Zuma with his penis showing. The only difference, it seems, is that a local Sunday newspaper treated the story of the portrait's creation earnestly, and so set in motion earnest, and eventually melodramatic, political and social responses. The newspaper is not to blame. Hasty responses from critics are the real tragedy here.

One of the most incredible refrains, for example, is the insistence that the office of the presidency deserves respect. Yet, a moment's reflection is all that is needed to make nonsense of this claim – despite the ease with which the words roll off the tongues of many. For one thing, it really is not clear what it means to respect the office of the presidency. I don't think critics mean that the physical building in which the president lives or works should be respected. It is rather odd to respect buildings. I think critics mean that the title of 'president' demands respect. But again, what is a title? How does one respect a title? Titles don't exist. They are just that – a title. In this case, the title means that the person called 'president' has certain constitutional powers that come with the title. But why should that fact mean that the current holder of the title must be respected as a matter of course? It is just plain weird to fetishise titles. I don't get it.

What makes much more sense to me is the idea that we should respect persons. And so perhaps what critics mean is something to the effect of, 'Always respect the person who is the current president of the Republic of South Africa.' At least now I am being asked to respect a person – rather than a building or a title.

But there is an obvious problem with this idea. Why must I respect someone just because they are the president of the country? That does not make sense either. Imagine, for example, being Zimbabwean, and weeping for the collapse of your country under the dictatorial weight of one Robert Mugabe, and being told you have to respect the man because he is the president of your country. I cannot respect a priest just because of his title, any more than I have to respect a headmaster just because of his title. Why, therefore, must I respect Jacob Zuma just because he is president?

Brett Murray is entitled, not just as an artist, but as a citizen, to disrespect the president of the country. If the president is to be respected, he must earn my respect. It is up to me to give respect, and to take respect away. I cannot be ordered to respect any human being unconditionally just because they have a title.

In this particular case, the inspiration for moral and political lampooning is clear. The president has had a colourful, prolific sexual life so far – one that appears to be continuing full steam ahead. I happen to support polygamy, so do not find that morally repugnant. But if the artist does, then the artist is entitled to comment on the perceived immorality, in this case by displaying the main 'weapon' around which polygamy is centred – the penis. We also know, of course, that the president has had unprotected sex outside of marriage. Again, this is not necessarily morally offensive for all of us, but many do find it offensive (even if they do so hypocritically). And so Brett Murray's work of art, if anything, is a rather unimaginative portrayal of the sexual ethics of the president. But the artist's entitlement to exhibit his take on the sexual morality of the president must be protected. Why else do we bother to constitutionally protect artistic freedom?

PENIS PASSION

The People's protest against Brett Murray is not only about the role of the artist in society. As I suggested in the opening line of this essay, it is also about our prudish attitudes towards nudity. It is the display of a penis, let's not forget, that has been the focus of the public outcry. We have similarly conservative attitudes towards the human body as you would find – to be fair on ourselves – around the world. Sexual organs are treated as dirty, embarrassing 'things'. To talk about these things is uncouth enough, but to put them on public display is the height – or low point – of depravity. That is the underlying attitude in public disapproval of this artwork.

The passion that this penis representation has unleashed simply tells us how Victorian we are. It does not necessarily tell us – one hopes – how opposed we are to freedom of expression. But in defending our prudishness we inadvertently trample on core democratic freedoms.

The real question, on this occasion, is why the penis is so scary? Some people responded to the artwork as if it were not an imitation of life but the president's actual penis that had been ripped from him and put on display. The fear of nudity is so strong that the fact that this is an artefact is something that seems to have escaped many.

All of this, of course, shows the need for art education so that the role of the artist, especially in a maturing democracy, can be understood and accepted. To constrain the artist politically is to constrain freedom of expression more generally. This is no way to promote and develop a deliberative democracy, a society in which there is a free flow of ideas.

But we also need to get over our fears of nudity. For a country that is battling with the scourge of HIV/AIDS, if we continue to regard the human body, in all its glory, as too dirty to be the subject of public discourse, including protest art, then we stand little chance of arresting wider, unhealthy attitudes towards sex. We therefore not only clamp down on Brett Murray in demanding his work of art be taken down. In the process, we also reinforce archaic attitudes towards sex and sexuality – do not talk about 'it'. 'It' is dirty, 'private' stuff only.

The penis is not all that special. Let's not cover it up and destroy artistic freedom in the name of preserving prudishness.

?

DO ANIMALS HAVE THE SAME ETHICAL
STATUS AS HUMANS?

WHY DO WHITES HAVE MEDICAL AID FOR THEIR
ANIMALS BUT NOT FOR THEIR MAID?

WHAT DO ANIMALS TEACH US ABOUT OURSELVES?

RHINOS ARE
PEOPLE TOO

One evening I asked my listeners what they thought about rhino poachers. What, I asked, could we do to stem the crisis of rhinos being killed around the country? The question prompted raw and deep emotion in the voices of my callers.

'Bring back the death penalty! Bring back the death penalty!' was the refrain. That was, by a long shot, my callers' preferred solution.

'Make an example out of one or two of the bastards and then they will stop!' And, just when I thought a sensible caller was bound to interrupt the death penalty chant by challenging others' empathy for rhinos as excessive, I got this: 'Eusebius, I do NOT think we should bring back the death penalty!' Phew! Finally. A sane voice among the death penalty madness, I prematurely thought. 'The death penalty is too easy Eusebius! I think we should rather let the bastards rot in jail for the rest of their lives!'

Now *that* took me by surprise. I thought the death penalty was harsh enough, but here was a caller trying to convince me that the death penalty was in fact a soft option.

This story raises an ethical question. Do animals have an ethical entitlement to be treated with the same level of respect as humans? I think the answer is a firm 'no'. For many South Africans the answer is 'yes'. Here's my argument for why I think those who say 'yes' are mistaken.

RHINOS HAVE FEELINGS
Some people think that animals and human beings have, or should have, equal moral status. Animals, for these people, are worthy of the same level of concern which other human beings demand of us.

The reason they think this is because we have interesting stuff in common with animals that suggests that animals deserve the same moral consideration as human beings. We have feelings. So do many, if not most, animals. A dog wagging its tail when it sees its master is a happy dog. Sure, animal emotions are not as interesting, as complex, and as wide-ranging as human emotions (perhaps), but at the absolute least, one might say that dogs have prototypes of human emotions.

And dogs are not an exception. Many other animals, from birds to horses to chimpanzees, make uncannily familiar noises, and display uncanny actions that resemble the kinds of noises we make, the kinds of actions and body language we exhibit, when we emote, from the moaning and groaning that accompanies sexual pleasure, to whistling as we walk down the road. We really just are animals, but complex, arrogant ones who think we are oh-so special.

So as far as the emotions business is concerned, humans and non-human animals have something important in common. This gives us good reason to have the same moral regard for animals as we do for humans. Or so the argument from the rhino brigade starts out.

A second commonality between humans and (other) animals is our capacity to experience pain and pleasure. This is the shared feature on which animal rights activists most often focus. Writing in the seventies and eighties, philosophers such as Peter Singer were particularly good at teasing out the moral implications of this common characteristic between us and other creatures.

We don't like pain. We like pleasure. The same goes for animals. Just as you do not want to be whacked over the head with a baseball bat because it hurts, so too a dog doesn't have a wish to be kicked, or stabbed, or hit over the head. And, just as it gives you warm and fuzzy feelings to have hubby stroke your back, so too your pet experiences a prototype of that kind of emotional satisfaction when you play with it. We are all 'sentient' creatures.

There are some exceptions or debatable cases. Many of my friends who are so-called vegetarian, for example, eat fish. Some of them justify this by claiming that fish do not have sufficiently complex nervous systems and are therefore not sentient creatures. They don't experience pain when caught on a hook. I do not know much about fish. But at least one can see the consistency in the reasoning here.

Let's accept, without contestation, the main claims I have tried to explain on behalf of the rhino brigade: a) non-human animals have feelings; and b) non-human animals are sentient. Does it follow that human beings and rhinos and dogs deserve the same moral consideration when I reason about them? No. Here's why.

FALSE MORAL EQUIVALENCE

One of the most intractable debates in moral discourse grapples with the question, 'Why should I act morally?' I can't answer that question comfortably, neither here or within an academic space. I have never come across a satisfying answer as a moral philosophy student and lecturer. Most of the debates in moral philosophy or ethics, if we are honest, proceed from the assumption that we all want to be moral – whatever that really means – and then get on with fights about what the correct moral theory is that we should follow.

But the nagging question about the point, and scope, of moral rules and moral theories comes back to haunt us when we debate animal rights. The rhino brigade gives us a legitimate headache. Why shouldn't we include animals in the scope of our moral reasoning? Furthermore, why shouldn't we regard them with the same level of concern as we do human beings?

My position, I admit upfront, is partly anthropocentric. By that I just mean that I have a bias towards humans – but one I will defend shortly – stemming from the fact that morality seems to be a peculiarly human affair. That, for me, is good enough reason to resist the demand that I should have the same moral regard for a rhino as I should for a human being.

First, it is important to get a sense of how my motivation to be moral works. My impulse to behave morally at all – don't ask whether I succeed all the time! – stems from the fact that other human beings and I have a lot in common, a lot more than just having feelings and being sentient. I have complex relationships with other human beings, including human beings who are different from me racially, linguistically, culturally, in class terms, and in all sorts of other ways. Other human beings are fundamentally like me.

Animal rights activists focus only on a few of the similarities between us and other animals. They don't focus on all of the differences, nor do they reflect hard enough on the implications of those differences for ethics. They also don't focus on all of the similarities between human beings.

I can't help but empathise with other human beings. This flows from the fact that we are of the same species. It is not hard for me to empathise with a beggar. It is very hard for me to empathise with a donkey. We give due moral regard to the interests of other human beings precisely because we are capable of feeling their plight. We can imagine being them. I can't imagine being a donkey. The lives of animals are alien to me. It is therefore odd to imagine that my moral duties towards my siblings, friends, colleagues, neighbours are the same, morally, as those I have for other animals.

And that is how I make sense of the business of morality. Yes, it is perhaps not, in a principled or logical sense, utterly satisfying. But it is where I am at, philosophically, in my reflection on morality. Empathy, it seems to me, is what kick-starts the pressure I place on myself, and others, to behave morally. But empathy, in this sense, works because other human beings are fundamentally like me. And that is what I mean by saying that morality is a peculiarly human affair. For this reason, I'm afraid, Mr Rhino is only second in line for being an object of concern to me after Mr Human Beggar, or Ms Human Stranger.

SOME OBVIOUS OBJECTIONS

Of course, some people will point out that many of us don't show empathy for other human beings but are still expected to give equal moral consideration to their interests. For example, many racists don't have regard for the interests of people from other race groups. But we don't say that for these racists there is no moral duty to treat other race groups like their own. We still demand that they regard all race groups as having equal moral status. If they don't, we rightly judge them as immoral!

So isn't it the same, one might say, with animals? Shouldn't we demand that everyone treats all animals morally, the same as they do humans, even if they don't or won't or struggle to? In other words, isn't it wrong of me to say that just because I empathise more easily with humans than with rhinos, that is enough reason to have greater regard for the interests of humans? That sounds, doesn't it, suspiciously like the way bigots reason all the time.

Not quite. This is actually an age-old objection, and one I used to find convincing when I was an undergraduate. But in the last few years I have changed my mind. I now think that the objection is just a little too quick, a little too neat. The analogy with racism isn't obviously convincing.

The racist is morally out of line because human beings with a different skin colour to theirs have the same complex social and psychological needs and profile. In other words, the discrimination against someone from another race group is arbitrary and irrational because of the rich similarities between people. The fundamental similarities between human beings run way too deep for me to get away with differentiating the needs of blue people from the needs of purple people. And by 'needs', I don't just mean having feelings, or hating pain, and generally enjoying pleasure: I mean being a social creature, falling in and out of love, enjoying social structures like familial life, linguistic and intellectual prowess and interactions, the ability to step back from the details of life's tapestry and being a reflective creature, having consciousness, experiencing complex emotional bonds and inner lives, and so on.

Many thinkers who have tried to defend my position, or a similar one, have sometimes made the mistake of saying things like, 'Human beings have consciousness but other animals don't!' or 'We can reason, and other animals can't!' Responses have rightly pointed out that this is not true of all human beings – like babies or mentally incapacitated persons – which would then mean that babies or some mentally ill patients, say, don't deserve the same moral consideration, presumably, as most fully grown persons? And so that spat has played out.

I am definitely not suggesting that there is one magic trait about humans that explains why I think humans deserve moral priority over other animals. I reject that position, in fact. I would rather say it is the irreducible combination of traits about us, that I described two paragraphs ago, that explains why I prioritise human beings in my moral reasoning.

And of course, yes, I have prejudices against other humans. (The first section of this book contains many such confessions of moral waywardness.) But the very reason that I try to root out my prejudices against other people is because we share such complex combinations of specifically human traits.

And that, ultimately, is why I think it is mad to regard rhinos as being people too, as it were ...

WHAT ABOUT ANIMAL CRUELTY?

To be clear, I think animal cruelty is immoral. It is wrong because animals are sentient. If human beings, as sentient creatures, do not want to experience pain, then it seems inconsistent and arbitrary to inflict pain on animals that also do not enjoy the experience of pain. None of this contradicts the argument I have developed all along.

My central point, all along, was simply that it is wrong to think that humans and non-humans have the same moral status. But I can think that Johan or Cecile is morally superior to the cat without thinking that it is morally acceptable to set the cat alight. My position is not a licence to treat animals badly. It is simply an argument for the relative, greater moral importance of human interests over those of other animals.

So where does this leave my relationship with animals? I happily eat braaied meat because I do not regard the beasts I am eating as having moral claims against me to exist. I only think members of my own species should not be eaten because they share so much more with me than do cows, as I have already explained. I am also, for the same reason, comfortable with the ritual slaughtering of animals, even in the suburbs.

Where I draw the line, however, is with rituals that do not respect the moral entitlement of sentient creatures to not experience unnecessary and excessive pain. This is why the bull-killing ritual of the Zulus, which happens annually, is immoral. The beast suffers immense and excessive pain, and yet it is a ritual that surely is dispensable. There must be other, non-cruel ways of culturally giving praise to ancestors or Mother Nature. So I am totally opposed to animal cruelty, and cultural rituals that involve the maltreatment of animals.

A POSTSCRIPT: CULTURAL OR RACIAL DIFFERENCES?

Despite my strong views on the moral status of animals, I am genuinely keen to make sense of why many of my radio callers feel so angry about rhino poachers that they would advocate the death penalty as a way of dealing with the crisis. And when I started reflecting on this difference between their attitude and mine, I wondered what role cultural and racial backgrounds and identities play in our attitudes towards animals? I went 'there' in search of an answer, perhaps predictably as a South African, but the search for an explanation steeped in identity and background differences, may well be relevant.

The other day I visited a good friend of mine, Thokozile, who lives a rather posh life in a hideaway somewhere quiet in Sandton. Every time I go to her place, which is part of a cluster of secured houses, I am surprised they haven't yet put up the sign, 'Pleasantville'. Her house is absolutely stunning, complete with birds chirping innocently in the garden as if greater Johannesburg were not a concrete mess competing for space with organisms. You just have to smile when you stand on Thokozile's porch, because Mother Nature slows you down, de-stresses you. And they say money can't buy you happiness ...

The only thing that could make my friend's neighbourhood the *really* perfect setting for an American middle class drama series like *Desperate Housewives* would be if a well-sculpted Latino gardener, scantily clad, were thrown into the mix. But perhaps I just didn't spot the bugger!

I asked her where Simba, her wonderful husband, was. And, true to Pleasantville form – and in anticipation of my predictable taunting to follow – she told me he was walking the dog! Ha ha.

I just had to laugh, and a conversation between everyone present (all of us black) started about the relationship different race groups, in general, have towards animals and pets. It wasn't just the fact that Simba was being rather middle class by strolling around the posh neighbourhood with the canine; it was also, for many of us, a rather un-black thing to do so.

'A friend of mine who is a filmmaker explored the issue. Because of the legacy of apartheid, many black South Africans are still scared of dogs!' said Lionel, one of my friends.

And he is right. Those black Alsatians used by apartheid cops did not exactly endear black South Africans to dogs. In fact, we didn't even know them as Alsatians. We simply referred to them as 'police dogs'. We thought that the breed was 'police dogs'. They were aggressive monsters that mauled us, terrorised us, and served their racist masters, the pawns of the apartheid system – cops – rather well.

This is also why a column by local newsreader, Nikiwe Bikitisha, in late 2010, resonated with many of her *Mail & Guardian* readers. While she was jogging around Zoo Lake in

Johannesburg she stopped in her tracks at the sight of a bull terrier not on the leash that its white owner had in her hand. When Nikiwe asked the woman to put the dog on a leash, she patronisingly told Nikiwe to be calm, since any hint of strong emotion would simply make the beast aggressive.

Of course, not only blacks are scared of a terrier on the loose. But, as Lionel had observed, blacks have memory of associating dogs with violence. And, so, while in one sense, Nikiwe's fear was not political – a terrier is a terrier – she recognised, some 20 years after Mandela's release, that her general attitude towards dogs remained shaped by apartheid. And whatever we think of these origins, one thing's for sure, and salient: blacks and whites, in general, have very different relationships with, and attitudes towards, dogs, and other animals. Exceptions to this generality exist – like Simba who walks his new canine friend around Pleasantville. But exceptions are just that.

When I discussed the issue on radio I knew it would be a matter of time before a black caller would have enough! Eventually an irate man from Alexandra called in, and said, 'Eusebius, you know ... eish... (*insert hearty chuckle*) ... these white people care more for animals than for human beings! Let me tell you something. Some of them even put the cat on medical aid! *The bloody cat!* You find even the money they leave behind when they die goes to that cat. But they can't put the maid on medical aid!'

I was practically on the floor with laughter! Some stereotypes, let's face it, contain really funny, and really true, nuggets of social truth. Of course the lines went crazy. The rhino brigade was mortally offended. A couple of blacks called in to say how much they love their pets to dispel the myth that blacks hate pets and animals. And some whites called in to assure me that they, too, are gatvol with the rhino brigade. It made for entertaining radio. But the exceptions do not change general differences in attitude.

The moral is this: I am mindful that my resistance to the idea that there is a moral equivalence between animals and humans might well be grounded in my own life's facts. People who connect with animals in profound ways may well have the kinds of rich relationships with them that I have with people. But, then again, I'm not sure I am capable of being so open-minded that I could seriously believe that an old white lady engages her pussy as satisfyingly as I do my friends, lovers or family!

What I am prepared to commit to, however, is the view that all sentient creatures deserve to be treated decently. Still, a well-raised cow, treated decently, and slaughtered swiftly and humanely, is more than welcome to appear as ribs, wors or steak on my dinner plate. Yum yum!

IS THERE ANYTHING WRONG WITH BEING A COCONUT?

_____

ARE FORMER WHITES-ONLY SCHOOLS REALLY
MULTICULTURAL?

_____

CAN'T BLACK KIDS ALSO LIKE ROCK?

_____

DON'T CALL ME COCONUT, BRU

Is it necessarily offensive to be called a 'coconut'? I once described myself as a coconut and an older friend of mine gently rebuked me, 'You're using the word at great cost to yourself.' I think he meant that my use of the word strikes him just as the word 'slut' would if a sex worker were to say it in reference to herself, or, if a black person were to say, 'I'm a kaffir.' I think that's what he means by the somewhat obscure phrase, 'at great cost to yourself'. The word 'coconut', for him, is so full of insult that there must be a kind of self-hate that comes with describing yourself as 'coconut', 'slut' or 'kaffir'. I wonder if he is right?

The more I reflect on the issue the more I think he is missing a bigger point. The debate about 'coconuts' is really about multicultural education. It centres on the question, 'Are former whites-only schools, especially the former model C ones, multicultural?'

The answer is 'no'. Black kids learn the social grammar of whiteness – hence the label 'coconut' – but there is little to no cross-cultural exchange in the other direction. Most white kids come out of those schools still knowing very little about the world beyond their predominantly white suburbs. These schools are mostly mono-cultural, frankly. The label 'coconut', for me, is a *usefully* contentious label, because it focuses attention on the pseudo-integration that has (not) happened in our schools, let alone in our wider communities, workplaces or other public spaces.

WHAT OR WHO IS COCONUT, ANYWAY?

I'm not sure what the precise origins of the 'coconut' label in South Africa are, but the term became popular during the early nineties when black kids started attending former whites-only schools. A 'coconut' is one of those black kids who speaks English 'so well' and with little hint of a township background. (Some even 'twang' unashamedly like erstwhile 'Zap Mag' presenter Vusi Twala, who surely is one of The Original Coconuts who went to Benoni High School.)

Coconuts also adopt a lot of the lingo, and not just accents, of their white friends – words like 'bru' suddenly flow out of beautiful thick black lips, and not only from thin little almost-lips on white skin.

My own vocab expanded quickly when I joined Graeme College Boys' High. The rules of grammar and formal vocabulary taught at the coloured primary school I had attended (St Mary's Primary) by my English teacher, Ms Jacobs, had to go. Ironically, non-mother tongue speakers often comply with the formal rules of English grammar better than native speakers. But in order to fit in at these schools, black kids quickly learn to break the grammar rules because the social rules say they must.

I quickly learned new words like 'oke' (as in, 'Okes, the bell has gone! Shut up and get in line for assembly!'), 'sarmie' (as in – usually from a matric boy to someone in standard six – 'Jason, go buy me a toasted cheese sarmie at the tuck shop'), 'co-ord' (often shouted at a clumsy, fat kid who misses a ball passed to him during physical education class), 'lank' (as in, 'I'm lank pissed off with you, dude') and 'dos' (as in, 'I need to dos [= nap] before we go out later'), all of which softened my formal vocabulary. Such is the making of a coconut! Even Afrikaans words like 'moer' and 'nooit' soon develop new shades of Anglicised meaning. ('I snogged Leanne at the social!' could, for example, get the jealous response, '*Nooit bru!*')

Besides language, there are other coconut markers, including clothing, music and other preferences that show the extent to which you have been acculturated in your new white setting. My own first coconut CD was Bon Jovi's 'These Days'. I listened to the title track again the other day and I must admit I feel that song deep in my bones, despite some rather dark lyrics: 'Jimmy's shoes busted both his legs, trying to learn to fly! From a second storey window, he just jumped and closed his eyes. His mama said he is crazy. He said, "Mamma I got to try! Don't you know that all my heroes died? And I guess I'd rather die than fade away!"'

Not exactly the stuff that a happy adolescence is made of. But that is one of the things that a coconut quickly learns – embracing white kids' teenage angst. I don't know how we rebel in the township. I guess you don't have much space to do so. Your mom will give you a fat *klap* if you get too cheeky. White kids, I quickly learned, express themselves by playing weird angry music loudly in their rooms. And groups like Bon Jovi helped them to vent. Some of the music from Green Day, and other much more hard rock stuff, seemed more popular among the white kids who were *particularly* angry at life!

As a black kid in these environments, you're only truly a coconut if you fully get the social grammar of white teenage angst, such as a white teenager's music selection! And thank God for that – I make no apologies for loving groups like Bon Jovi, Green Day and Red Hot Chilli Peppers. I cannot, though, say the same of Guns N' Roses – those dudes simply produced noise, even though I had to put up with it at my school hostel.

Kids who grew up in the township, rather than spending half their days in white schools, didn't need to negotiate this complex social grammar. Coconuts are experts at whiteness: both the literal language of their white peers, and the social grammar. And, boy, how well we mimic.

LEARNING TO BE PRECOCIOUS: A GREAT HIDDEN CURRICULUM

Less easy to pin down are the values that were inculcated in black kids at these former model C schools. Values are not particularly tangible things – they are principles you are committed to and live your life by, and they tend to be revealed in your actions, your character disposition, your beliefs, your attitudes, etc. And one really has to look at the narrative of someone's entire life, or a good chunk of it, before you can have a go at saying what some of their values are.

In my experience, kids at white schools were more assertive, more willing to challenge authority, than many of us were who had come from township schools. They had a very strong sense of individualism and entitlement. Many of the black kids, by contrast, were often from primary school backgrounds where we looked up to our teachers to such an extent that there was a clear vertical power relationship which scared the living daylights out of us. Teachers were feared rather than respected. My new white teachers, on the other hand (with the exception of Mr Van der Meulen, the physical education teacher) had no such luck. They had to earn the respect of these precocious, confident white brats who behaved as if the world owed them something.

This quickly rubbed off on us too. We also had to learn to be assertive, and in my view this constitutes one of the biggest positive contributions that these schools made to the lives of those black kids who could afford to attend them – it helped those of us from backgrounds in which authority is structured vertically to learn to find our own voices in the classroom, and to slowly become irritatingly assertive middle class types (in a good way). This, too, was part of the white grammar that coconuts were taught. A coconut, unlike his township counterpart, is generally a more confident, more assertive creature. And that's cool.

All schools have a 'hidden curriculum'. This is not the official stuff that is taught in the classroom. It is the stuff that happens when the teacher is off duty, but not quite off duty, such as when the teacher is chatting to the pupils while driving them to a sporting event at a rival school, or perhaps while on a long journey to a music festival in another city. During these 'off' moments, you can affect the character and personal development of a learner much more than when you are standing in front of the class. Equally, the general behaviour of staff and the institution's attitude towards such things as learners who make mistakes, how it handles discipline, etc., are all facts about the school's hidden curriculum. These elements can profoundly shape future adults, sometimes more so than rote-learning facts in class.

And, in my opinion, the single most positive difference between going to former whites-only schools and township schools is that black kids, in general, emerge a little more arrogant from former model C schools, with that middle class sense that the world owes them something. This is *not* a bad thing at all.

As a debate coach, and a mentor to some younger South Africans, I often realise that half my mental energy has to be focused on instilling a sense of self-belief in young black South

Africans, even in those learners and students who are self-evidently skilled or have the potential to be utterly brilliant. There is a massive deficit in self-belief, no doubt owing to our apartheid past, which left black people's self-confidence – still – shattered. And model C schools do not get enough credit for the invaluable contribution they make – even if only a few black kids benefit – to instilling in young black children a sense of can do-ism, a sense of confidence that they can make it.

And this is why I think the term 'coconut' is not only derisive, but also contains some positive stuff. Truth be told, we'd be better off as a country if there were more, not fewer, coconuts around.

DIFFERENCES WILL PERSIST

I did feel sorry, though, for our families. They suddenly had to deal with assertive black kids who thought the world owed them something. In fact, I was sometimes even told by kids in my own neighbourhood (who obviously had not attended model C schools), *'Jy hou jou wit!'* ('You think you're white!') This was partly innocent jealously that I was at a better school than the local alternative where coloured kids would normally go. It was also, however, recognition of the fact that I now carried myself with a sense of pride, a sense of going places, a sense of conviction that my future was not to be found in the downtrodden community where I was born and raised. This confidence all stems from the fact that I found my voice at Graeme College Boys' High, my sense of individualism, and self-belief that not only did I owe it to myself to be the best that I could be in life, but actually I had a *duty* towards myself to make the most of the opportunities life had offered me.

But, rather comically, I quickly discovered the limits of this precociousness! I had to be a different animal at home from what I was at school. There's nothing like the imprint of your mom's, dad's, brother's, or uncle's or aunt's five fingers on your teenage cheek to bring you literally and figuratively down to Earth if you were being a cocky wanna-be white kid at home. You were still just a kid in the house, and only when the family wanted to brag about you to a visitor, were you allowed to gloat about your white school experiences. Beyond that, you were to be treated more or less like the kids who were not at your school.

This means that coconuts have to be particularly nifty at wearing different hats. We could not easily be our assertive coconut selves at home. White kids, on the other hand, had it easy – they could be their normal, authentic selves both at home and at school. They did not have to play the same kinds of social identity games that black kids had to play, negotiating two worlds. White kids lived in the same world in which the school was located. This wasn't the case for black kids, and so we had to wear different hats at different times of the day. The results, though, could be awkward.

I remember my embarrassment once when a friend called me while I was at home and I spoke to him in English. My little cousin could not stop giggling while listening to me 'being white' on the phone! I simply had to grin and bear it. But I didn't give my number out to any other white friends after that. The embarrassment was something of a double whammy: a cousin laughing at me speaking English but, also, the phone being answered by someone in my family responding in incorrect English to my white friend at the other end!

Such is the personal struggle of coconut teenagers: a private reality filled with complexities that you keep to yourself and hope to carefully manage like a good piece of choreography.

It was also very instructive visiting white friends. You can imagine my shock when I first discovered how my first white

friend, Andrew, and his sister, Sarah, related to their mother.
I went to Andrew's house to play chess. He had introduced me
to the game. And I became hooked. His room was messy and
full of posters. I did not have a room of my own at home but if
I did there would be no way in hell it could be this messy! But
white parents seem to somehow think that teenagers are adults
who should be 'given space', a very odd concept for me. But one
particular afternoon a bigger shock awaited me while Andrew
and I were in his room playing a chess match.

Suddenly, there came some distracting shouting and
screaming from elsewhere in the house. An older female voice
was competing with a much younger, offensively shrill one.
Andrew looked embarrassed, but continued to set the pieces,
trying hard to be blasé about it all.

'Sarah! Come over here, right now! You cannot leave these
things draped everywhere!'

'Stop fucking shouting at me, Shirley!' came the shrill voice
in response, before a door slammed.

That was my introduction to the ongoing screaming matches
between mother and daughter. I was shocked. Not that such
verbal violence did not happen at my place. God forbid, it was
worse! My mom often hurled ashtrays at my sisters and me. But
the rules of engagement in the township were *very* different. You
would sooner be seen slapping your mother than calling her by
her first name!

Somehow, even the worst fights between my mother and
sisters were rehearsed within the semblance of respect for the
parent-child relationship. The closest they would come to de-
cloaking my mom of her status as matriarch would be to say,
rather pathetically, 'You are not my mother!' Even then, they
risked hilarity from the by-standing crowd watching the fight,
because it would be a truly pathetic jab. The township parent-

child relationship withstands any domestic squabble! However, to go from, 'You are not my mother!' to 'I hate you, Magdalene!' would have catapulted my sisters straight into hell. It would be worse than any physical injury.

In Andrew's world, things were different. You could use violence as a last resort (and even then dispense with the ashtrays and choose something more dramatic, like family suicide) but, in the meantime, do scream and shout at *Shirley* – not Mother – to your heart's content! I have little doubt that my sisters would have earned that familiar, decisive, consciousness-challenging, snot *klap* if they played the domestic violence game by such unethical rules as Sarah.

In many ways my unfolding friendship with Andrew was random, as, I guess, childhood experiences are, for the most part – a casual greeting leading to mutual interests in running, fantasy novels, competitive chess, rock music, maths Olympiads … looking back now, the influence was all one way, however. I was entering the white world, the white world resisted coming to the township.

Andrew, my first white friend, one of my best friends at school, had never visited my grandparents' home, never visited my mother's house. He never asked. And I never invited him.

THE PROBLEM WITH COCONUTS AND MODEL C SCHOOLS

My friendship with Andrew illustrates the general problem. There never really was genuine multicultural integration in model C schools. I lived in Andrew's world. Andrew did not live in mine. He lived *around* my world. I visited his maternal and paternal grandparents' houses regularly. His dad's parents, in particular, were very fond of me, and I felt like their grandchild, in fact. And, beyond that, his dad, his mom and stepmom got to know me very well. I was such a 'normal' part of their life that I can honestly say that I felt part of the family. Racial differences, despite my observations here, were not, in the domestic details of those experiences, foregrounded. Andrew's stepmom, Janet, for example, was a political animal, and simply responded to me as she would a son interested in current affairs and politics (which Andrew was not into.) Even now, some two decades later, his stepmom and I chat up a storm whenever we bump into each other.

But, when I reflect back, on that childhood, and high school multicultural experiment, I have to conclude that ultimately it was one-way traffic: me learning how to negotiate white South Africa. Andrew remained in that world. He was *from* there. We were just kids. No-one is to blame. But our implicit decision to play out our friendship in his world only, does reflect just how hegemonic white norms are in South Africa, despite demographic shifts in many of the former whites-only schools.

Of course I could have invited him home. But I didn't. I was ashamed of my poor neighbourhood. Language, class and race divisions all combined to make me skilled at wearing different hats, negotiating different worlds rather than integrating them.

This is the only – but no small – problem with coconuts, and former model C schools. There is nothing wrong with confident young black men and women taking the world by storm while listening to Bon Jovi. That's fine. But if the bigger aim in South Africa is that we get to know each other's worlds intimately and genuinely, then we need to dispel the myth that we have a cluster of schools – private schools and former model C ones – that are templates worth repeating elsewhere. That is not true. These schools, instead, should be doing some soul-searching and grappling with why it is that they are closed to the diverse linguistic, cultural, and class backgrounds of their learner population. The leadership in these schools often does not reflect on the unintended consequences of simply thinking that it was all 'business as usual' when they opened their doors to learners from different backgrounds.

In fact, they ought to have thought about, and revised, their 'hidden curricula'. It is not too late. But it will take effort. A once-a-year 'cultural day' when some Xhosa kids bring pap to school for their white friends is a patronising effort. Deeper cultural and normative changes are needed so that there is an equality of cultural identities accommodated and celebrated in our schools throughout the year.

This matters deeply: schools are not just places where we learn to read, write and count. They are places where our personalities, characters and values are shaped. So we owe it to ourselves to re-engineer our educational spaces to produce genuinely multicultural citizens.

WHY DO WE LAUGH SO MUCH?
_____

ARE THERE LIMITS TO OUR LAUGHTER?
_____

ARE COMEDIANS THE NEW SOCIAL CONSCIENCE?
_____

THE FUNNY
REVOLUTION

South Africa has been experiencing something of a comedy revolution over the past few years. Stand-up comedy has surely never been more popular. And even film and television programmes starring local comedians and exploring comedy are thriving. This raises the question: why is there a successful funny revolution in our land?

There are, in my view, three reasons for comedy's success: laughing is a coping mechanism for us; all of us enjoy seeing ourselves narrated in the arts; and comedy allows us, being rainbow nation-obsessed, to laugh in national unison.

GREAT COMEDY?

The techniques our comedians use to evoke the laughter in us are many and varied of course.

A couple of years ago I took a few friends from overseas to a weekly comedy evening at Blues Room at The Village Walk in Sandton. The comedy club used to be hosted by Trevor Noah, during the days when he was not yet a rock star. Since then, Trevor has moved on to bigger and better things. The club, meanwhile, has gone under, but many more have mushroomed in big cities across the country.

On this particular Tuesday evening I was with two friends I had met at Oxford, one from Turkey and the other British. Boy, were they in for a surprise! The main act was Loyiso Gola. He really pushed the boundaries, sparing no race group, sexual creature, stereotype about what city in South Africa you were from, and much more. His funny bone was also well lubricated judging by the beer in his hand, and so the comedian's ego was even bigger than usual.

'Yeah, man, about the Olympics!' he said. 'We are useless, Joe … *useless*!!!!!!' Fair enough, I thought. South Africa does not exactly have an addiction to Olympic medals. We do horrendously badly. The only thing we can lay claim to is being consistent. Consistently bad.

'I mean … at least a darkie brought back a medal! Did you see that guy in the – fuck I don't know – long jump or triple jump? That guy can jump, Joe!'

I often wonder who 'Joe' is but I dare not show how unhip I am. I guess it would be a bit like wondering who Bob is when an Englishman says, 'And Bob's your uncle!' Anyway, the darkie with the medal, of course, was Khotso Mokoena. He got a silver medal at the Beijing Olympics in 2008.

'You whites are fucking useless!' Loyiso continued. I looked at my friends. They weren't yet uncomfortable but I could see they were getting just a tad restless.

'You whites are supposed to be able to swim and you could not even clean up in the swimming events! *Even … even*, Joe, when you had a competitive advantage. What's the name of the white chick with one leg? Uh … Natalie du Toit, ja! She had a great advantage over other swimmers and still could not win. She was, like, competing in some, I think they call it, open water event out in the ocean or something. All the swimmers were nervous. She wasn't. She knew the sharks would never come for her 'cause they prefer full portions to half portions. And *still* she could not win! Eish ...'

There were shocked gasps from sections of the audience. Many had their mouths covered, but by and large there was a *huge* round of sustained laughter and even those with mouths covered, chuckled. My two Oxonian friends, by contrast, were throwing glances at each other which suggested that this particular joke might have crossed the line. We only stayed a little while longer.

This example is both typical and atypical. It is typical in the sense that South African comedians really do not think much about what subject matter might not be appropriate. The aim is to extract laughter at all cost, sometimes even at the expense of a person's or group's dignity.

It is also atypical, to be fair on our comedians. It is not the case that anything goes. It is perhaps more accurate to say that we have a higher tolerance for inappropriate material than elsewhere. But there are some boundaries, some self-censoring. I hear very few jokes, for example, that explore the fears of some about what might happen when Mandela dies. Mandela's mortality seems to be a no-go area for many comedians, even though there is some rich material there about our attitude towards death, our relationship with the man and the myth, and the irrational fears of some about what will happen the morning after.

But South African comedy is more risky in subject matter and tone than comedy elsewhere. The reason? Because we are one of the most stressed-out nations outside of war zones, we are prepared to dig even deeper than other nations to make ourselves laugh. This is the effect of comedy as-coping mechanism.

SOCIAL COMMENT

It is easy not to take comedians very seriously. Many of us see them as the equivalent of street magicians, tricksters who make us laugh and are deserving of our small change. In reality, however, our best local comedians don't just help us cope with life in this stressful country; they are also excellent social commentators.

Let's go back to that Natalie du Toit joke. Trevor Noah came to Loyiso's rescue as the MC, keeping the flow going between the different acts. It does help that he is super charming, very attractive, and the most thoughtful comedian we have had in many years. Sometimes, in fact, his jokes are less like humour than fairly straight social comment. After Loyiso's act, Trevor looked at the audience and smiled. 'You guys can't believe, *ne*! You can't believe he was so *tjatjarag* as to make fun of a disabled person! ... Well, let me ask you this. Why not?! I crack a joke about Shangaans ... You laugh! I crack a joke about Cape Town coloureds ... You laugh! I crack a joke about gays ... You laugh! But, no, disabled people ... *hayibo* ... they can't be human like us, *ne*?!'

The audience chuckled. It wasn't raucous laughter, but smiles that ran away on their faces – he had challenged them gently, and provocatively. Loyiso was bad cop. Trevor was good cop. But both, in fact, had seriously encouraged the audience members to reflect on their attitude towards the disabled.

And this is why I love South African comedians. Besides the fact that I wouldn't mind having Trevor Noah's babies, he is an absolutely on-point social commentator. There is a profound intelligence that runs throughout his work that speaks of an incisive, critical mind.

CLASS ANXIETY

South African comedians also reflect back at us changes to our social dynamic. It is interesting to note how the material of comedians has evolved in recent years. There is now a lot of comment on class anxieties. Of course South Africa does not, in absolute terms, have a massive black middle class. But it exists, and it is growing. So many black comedians have grown up in former whites-only schools, and are professional and fairly cosmopolitan. But it means that many of them grapple with how to negotiate different aspects of their identity.

The idea of the coconut kid who is happy to turn his back on 'kulcha' is a lie. Black kids who go to former whites-only schools negotiate their ethnic, linguistic and cultural backgrounds in complex ways that we do not always pay close attention to. My teenage brother, for example, is at an English-medium, former whites-only school in Port Elizabeth. It has been fascinating for me to watch how he deals with these issues. (In 'Don't call me coconut, bru' I explore these identity questions more fully.) Many young comedians on the funny scene these days also explore these issues – they have less to do with race (although race is always in the background, of course, this being South Africa) and more to do with class tensions.

The starkest example – though it wasn't particularly funny – was when a young comedian, Mamello Mokoena, recently got onstage at a new comedy venue, Metro, in Sandton. He started speaking very fast, and in a thick township accent that was difficult to make sense of to the untrained middle class ear, and the audience started cringing within seconds. He was black, and most of the audience was black, but it was clear that he was an outsider in that space. And then, after what felt like ten minutes of gaffes, but which probably was really three minutes or so, he announced, 'That wasn't me, motherfuckers! I have a beautiful private school accent too!' There was a palpable sense of relief!

Funnily enough, most folks in the venue seemed to be black professionals but it wasn't obvious that most of them were necessarily private school educated. There are still only a handful of South Africans who can afford to attend top private schools, so this comedian still felt a little out of place, but this time not so much because he seemed like a poor lad who did not belong here, but because he now came across as an arrogant git who thought going to a private school (Redhill in his case) – as opposed to, say, a former model C school – was the ultimate social experience.

But here's the point: there was desperation in this comedian to explore, and even to show off, his class status as a privileged black guy who spoke very well, who had an elite education, and who could now confidently map his own career trajectory and go for gold. He suffered from class anxiety, quite frankly. And it is debatable whether he succeeded in holding a mirror to the audience, or whether he was holding up a mirror to himself. Still, this is a class motif that is becoming more popular in local comedy, and a comedic archive of the trials and tribulations of the emerging black middle class.

This class motif is an indication of how much local South African comedians draw on personal – and collective – biography in crafting their material. And this is the reason why our local comedy makes for such excellent social comment. Because comedians are not alien to our communities, but *from* our communities, and located *within* our communities, their jokes are filled with nuggets of social insight and reflections on social change in which we can all see ourselves.

When he first started out, for example, comedian Eugene Khoza recycled jokes of township girls one brings to posh restaurants in the north of Joburg only to be embarrassed by their inability to pronounce fancy words on the menu like *Filet Mignon*! He used to embellish the story with tales of their sheer amazement at some of the gadgets in the townhouses that their boyfriends would take them to, like the 'big flat screen TV!' Even those of us who had heard the joke countless times, still chuckled. And of course what we were chuckling at was the familiarity of class anxiety – how to behave in the suburbs, Joe?!

A new local film explores this technique of drawing on biography and personal identity as comedic subject matter. A comedy drama starring the brilliant Riaad Moosa, entitled *Material*, hit the circuit recently. It tells the story of a young Muslim man working in his dad's shop in Fordsburg. He secretly dabbles in stand-up comedy and his dad, when he finds out, is not amused, being conservative, but also having lost his sense of humour in the struggle against apartheid and in his feud with a sibling. It is an absolutely brilliantly film, and one in which the main character bears many resemblances to Riaad Moosa.

What struck me in particular when I twitterviewed Riaad – an interview on Twitter – was how insightful he was about his own art. Many artists are poor or mediocre when it comes to reflecting on, and speaking about, their craft, often resorting to banalities like 'music chose me' or 'the characters in my novels write themselves'. In Riaad I found plain but thoughtful reflection. He shared with me, for example, just how difficult he finds the South African comedy scene with all its hedonism (my word choice). He is a devout Muslim, and a qualified medical doctor, who simply loves cracking jokes. So in his own profession he has had to square a commitment to his religion with the reality of a work environment that is not always in keeping with the cultural and religious tenets of his own heritage and personal identity.

In fact, at one of the theatres where he once performed, he paid the manager to not sell alcohol on the premises when he was performing. Yet, this does not mean that he has sleepless nights about the ethics of his craft. He believes, like his counterpart in

Material, that no particular race, religious or cultural group has exclusive rights to laughter, or to making others laugh. And this is why it was a stroke of genius, in the casting for *Material*, for the filmmakers to choose local comedian Nik Rabinowitz to play the role of the comedy mentor. Nik pretty much starred as himself, and as a member of the Jewish community he has also shown that just because you come from a community that is often hastily reduced to difficult and intractable religious and political fault lines does not mean that you cannot be in the funny business.

COMEDY'S PURPOSE

So why is comedy thriving in South Africa? One reason, as I've said, is that comedy is a coping mechanism for us. We laugh at our traumatic past. And we laugh at the traumas and imperfections of post-democratic South Africa. Being hijacked or smash-and-grabbed is horrible. It is not less unacceptable when it is turned into comedy material, but there can be little doubt that it is good for your sanity, and for your immune system, to learn to deflate the anxiety and post-traumatic stress. Laughter is a healthy way of responding to our historic and present-day challenges – part escapism, part coping mechanism.

There is another reason we love comedy. In comedy we get to see ourselves – comedic moments feed off a desire in us to recognise ourselves in the work of the comedian. This is a social need human beings have, the need to be affirmed, to be recognised and to be acknowledged (even if you get lampooned). When I saw *Material*, for example, the theatre was packed with Indians, many of them wearing Muslim garb, including some very elderly people who seemed like they had been bused to the theatre for the occasion. This was not the crowd you would see at a Leon Schuster film in December. It is a crowd that obviously expected a film about a Muslim family to explore motifs familiar to them.

Of course there were moviegoers from different backgrounds, but I saw the film twice and on both occasions the audience was predominantly Indian, and seemingly largely Muslim.

It is equally unsurprising that many audiences at a Marc Lottering show are coloured – we want to see our life narratives reflected in the arts.

Perhaps most importantly for us South Africans, however, comedy gives us yet another chance at mythmaking. South Africa is a more deeply divided society than we like to accept. (I explore these differences in 'A divided nation'.) But we get anxious just talking about the subject. We fear it will take us back to a divided past. And so we desperately latch onto events, symbols and activities that seem to transform the myth of a united nation into reality. This is why we love big sporting events, for example – these often act as a temporary social cohesive that helps us all to get along nicely, like smarties in a smarties box.

We also unite in our laughter. When Trevor does his skit about South Africans from each racial and linguistic grouping struggling with some part of the national anthem, it lampoons us all, equally, but also allows us to laugh in unison. We laugh as a nation.

For me, this is one of the deeper psycho-social reasons for the funny revolution's success. Humour, like rugby and *koeksisters*, has become recognisably South African.

Long after Tutu's death it will be laughter – genuine, absurd or tragicomic – that will keep the rainbow nation myth alive.